RELIGIOUS DEVIANCE IN THE ROMAN WORLD

Religious individuality is not restricted to modernity. This book offers a new reading of the ancient sources in order to find indications for the spectrum of religious practices and intensified forms of such practices only occasionally denounced as "superstition". Authors from Cicero in the first century BCE to the law codes of the fourth century CE share the assumption that authentic and binding communication between individuals and gods is possible and widespread, even if problematic in the case of divination or the confrontation with images of the divine. A change in practices and assumptions throughout the imperial period becomes visible. It might be characterized as "individualization" and it informed the Roman law of religions. The basic constellation – to give freedom of religion and to regulate religion at the same time – resonates even into modern bodies of law and is important for juridical conflicts today.

JÖRG RÜPKE was Chair of Comparative Religion at the University of Erfurt from 1999 to 2015 and is now permanent Fellow for Religious Studies at the Max Weber Center. He is also co-director of the Research Group "Religious Individualization in Historical Perspective" and director of the ERC research project "Lived Ancient Religion". Since 2012 he has been a member of the German Council of Science and Humanities ("Wissenschaftsrat") and since 2013 Vice-Director of the Max Weber Center. His authored books include *Rituals in Ink* (2004); *The Religions of the Romans* (2007); *Fasti sacerdotum* (2008); *The Roman Calendar from Numa to Constantine: Time, History, and the Fasti* (2011); *Religion in Republican Rome: Rationalization and Ritual Change* (2012); *Ancients and Moderns: Religion* (2013); and *From Jupiter to Christ* (2014). He has also edited *Religion and Law in Classical and Christian Rome* (co-edited with Clifford Ando, 2006); *A Companion to Roman Religion* (2007); *Reflections on Religious Individuality* (2013); and *A Companion to the Archaeology of Religion in the Ancient Mediterranean* (co-edited with Rubina Raja, 2015).

RELIGIOUS DEVIANCE IN THE ROMAN WORLD

Superstition or Individuality?

JÖRG RÜPKE

REVISED AND ENLARGED EDITION,
TRANSLATED BY

DAVID M. B. RICHARDSON

CAMBRIDGE
UNIVERSITY PRESS

CAMBRIDGE
UNIVERSITY PRESS

University Printing House, Cambridge CB2 8BS, United Kingdom

Cambridge University Press is part of the University of Cambridge.

It furthers the University's mission by disseminating knowledge in the pursuit of
education, learning and research at the highest international levels of excellence.

www.cambridge.org
Information on this title: www.cambridge.org/9781107090521

This book was originally published in German by Mohr Siebeck in 2011 and was originally
known as *Aberglauben oder Individualität: Religiöse Abweichung im römischen Reich*.

© Jörg Rüpke 2016

This English translation © David M. B. Richardson 2016

First published 2011

This English language edition 2016

Printed in the United States of America by Sheridan Books, Inc.

A catalogue record for this publication is available from the British Library

Library of Congress Cataloguing in Publication data
Names: Rüpke, Jörg, author.
Title: Religious deviance in the Roman world : superstition or individuality? /
Jörg Rüpke; revised and enlarged edition, translated by
David M. B. Richardson.
Other titles: Aberglauben oder Individualität. English
Description: English language edition. | New York : Cambridge University
Press, 2016. | Includes bibliographical references and index.
Identifiers: LCCN 2016004911 | ISBN 9781107090521
Subjects: LCSH: Rome – Religion. | Religion and sociology – Rome. |
Free thought – Rome. | Deviant behavior – Rome. | Superstition – Religious
aspects. | Superstition – Rome. | Individualism – Religious aspects. | Social norms.
Classification: LCC BL805 .R8713 2016 | DDC 200.937–dc23
LC record available at http://lccn.loc.gov/2016004911

ISBN 978-1-107-09052-1 Hardback

Contents

Preface

The character of ancient Mediterranean religion of the Hellenistic and Imperial periods has come under debate. Rather than stressing the public, political, and collective character of what is frequently conceptualized as "pre-Christian" (or rather extra-Judaeo-Christian) religion(s), a number of recent studies have highlighted emotional and dynamic aspects, discourse and belief, the individual and the network within which he or she functions. Julia Kindt and Esther Eidinow, for instance, have offered observations and concepts in respect of the religion of Greek cities; members and guests of the Religious Individualization in Historical Perspective and Lived Ancient Religion research groups at Erfurt have done the same for Republican as well as Imperial Roman religion.[1] Evidently, the discussion is not only about adding a feature to the model of *polis* or civic religion, but about replacing that model as the primary mode of description. This brings methodological[2] and theoretical consequences.[3] The debate is far from resolved.[4] The present book follows just one facet of that debate, but an important one: the problem of individual religious behaviour at or beyond the margins of general approval. As it turns out, the concept of deviance and the evidence of behaviour called deviant offer an important insight both into public religious norms and into the primacy and persistence of individual religious experience and claims built upon it.

---

[1] Eidinow 2007, 2011, 2013; Kindt 2009, 2012; Rüpke and Spickermann 2012; Cusamano et al. 2013; Kracke, Roux, and Rüpke 2013; Rüpke 2013a, 2013b; Rüpke and Woolf 2013; Rüpke 2014a, 2014b.
[2] See Raja and Rüpke 2015.
[3] As outlined in Rüpke 2015a and more generally *Religion 45* (2015), issue 1.
[4] See, in particular, Scheid 2013.

Acknowledgements

This book owes its origin to two circumstances, each of which calls for my gratitude. First, I should like to give heartfelt thanks to the Collège de France for its gracious invitation to treat the theme of religious deviance in the context of a Guest Professorship in February and March of 2010. This provided me with an entire month to concentrate fully on developing the manuscript, and, in the course of four lectures, the opportunity to investigate the question of religious deviance in ancient Rome. To be able to do this in the presence of John Scheid was a source of particular pleasure for me. It was he who invited me to Paris for the first time, twenty years ago, on that occasion to work in the Sciences Religieuses section at the École Pratique des Hautes Études. It is also to him that I owe particular thanks for the invitation to the Collège de France. For the completion of the German manuscript, an invitation to a Guest Professorship at the Faculty of Theology of the University of Aarhus gave me a period of undisturbed work in a stimulating atmosphere; for this I owe especial thanks to Anders Klostergaard Petersen, for his critical reading of the completed text and his many suggestions.

For intensive discussions during the very much longer development phase, I thank the members of research group FOR 1013 of the Deutsche Forschungsgemeinschaft (DFG) at the Max Weber College for Cultural and Sociological Studies at Erfurt University, in particular Clifford Ando, Martin Fuchs, Richard Gordon, Dietmar Mieth, Wolfgang Spickermann, and Greg Woolf. Can religion be a medium of individualization? Under what conditions does religion achieve this? How can religious activity provide a context for individualization, for the development of individuality? When, and under what conditions, do religious institutions (understood in a broad sense) secure individualization in the long term, or perpetuate it? How do assumptions about the collective character of religion inform academic historical narratives? These questions posed by the Erfurt research group Religious Individualization in Historical Perspective, together with the problem of their application to the religions of ancient cities and societies, have formed the basis for the themes discussed in this book. The group has proved to be a productive vehicle of intellectual exchange; it was encouraged and enabled in its pursuit of a variety of topics by generous funding from the DFG, the necessary framework having been created with the support of the University of Erfurt, and in particular Bettina Hollstein and Diana Püschel. I offer my heartfelt thanks to all.

Selected translations from Tertullian are taken from Tertullian, Minucius Felix, translated by T. R. Glover and Gerald H. Rendall, Loeb Classical Library Volume 250, first published 1931, and used with permission. Loeb Classical Library® is a registered trademark of the President and Fellows of Harvard College.

I am grateful to Cambridge University Press for offering me the opportunity to review and consolidate my argument. The additional chapters and arguments were made possible by the ERC Advanced Grant "Lived Ancient Religion" (no. 295555 within the 7th Framework Programme funded by the European Union). Heartfelt thanks go again to David Richardson for his careful reading and translation.

CHAPTER I

Superstitio: *conceptions of religious deviance in Roman antiquity*

Starting point

What does religious deviance comprise? In a collection of practice speeches, perhaps originating in the early second century CE, and later ascribed to the celebrated teacher of rhetoric Quintilian (d. about 100 CE), the following fictional case (*Declamatio minor* 323) provides the basis for the plea by the accused. When Alexander the Great attacked Athens, he burned down a temple lying outside the walls of the city (the writer does not take the trouble to link the temple with a particular deity). The anonymous deity wrought revenge by sending a plague over the Macedonian army. Through the medium of an oracle, Alexander learns that the epidemic will end only when the temple is re-established. Alexander complies with the oracle's judgement, and rebuilds the temple more splendid than before. But rebuilding the temple is not enough: it has to be formally dedicated to the deity and consecrated. Regarding the sacred procedure to be followed, the writer quite specifically refers to Roman practice. Alexander wins over an Athenian priest with the promise to withdraw after the dedication. The priest agrees, and Alexander keeps to the agreement. And now comes the twist by which the story turns into a legal case: the priest is charged with having aided the enemy (*hosti opem tulisse*).

That this criminal case is replete with religion is a factor that the author's commentary does not neglect to emphasize. What interested the budding jurists and orators over the space of many pages need not concern us here. But how does the priest talk himself out of the charge, and – literally – save his neck? His final plea is based on the premise that if, in war, one does something that also indirectly helps the enemy, this cannot be construed *per se* as aiding the enemy (*opem ferre*). What is of interest to us is that the priest follows the logic of the religious norm: the Athenian god is angry; he demands a temple; so everything must be done in order to satisfy that desire. That the priest in addition compels the foe to withdraw must weigh in his favour, rather than his being blamed for the succour given to the opposing army. This is a case where a (seeming) military norm is departed from on the basis of religion; the question is primarily one of conflict between different norms, collision between different fields of practice. The author, writing much later under the Empire, is able to imagine that strict adherence to religious norms can lead to conduct that is seen in the wider social context as deviant.

At about the same time, the Greek philosopher Plutarch, who died in the twenties of the second century CE, was occupied with another case of religious deviance, also anonymous. But Plutarch's sights were set, not on the intellectual interest of an oratorical exercise, but on typifying an entire set of instances. A "superstitious" individual (*deisidaimonos*) would actually like to celebrate the cycles of festivals like anyone else; he would like to savour life and enjoy himself: but he cannot (*On Superstition* 9 = 169 D–E). Just as the temple is filled with the scent of incense, his soul is filled with supplications and laments. He has the festive wreath on his head, but he is pale; he sacrifices, but is afraid; he prays, but his voice trembles; he offers up incense, but his hands shake. As a measure of his own assessment of the case, Plutarch cites an observation ascribed to the ancient philosopher Pythagoras: proximity to the gods should bring out the best in us. But this man enters a temple as if it were a lion's den. To summarize this contemporary of the anonymous follower of Quintilian: to adopt religious norms to excess is to go a step too far. Behaviour that does not amount to criminality in legal terms is aberrant or deviant when viewed from a religious perspective.

What the two instances have in common is the surprising third-party perspective, the outrage, the shift of norms that is required in order to make religious behaviour deviant. This book thus embarks upon a dual journey. By investigating deviance and infringements of norms, I intend to identify actual variations in religious behaviour. To what extent did individuality exist in the religious sphere in antiquity? Must the accepted view of the collective character of pre-modern religion be called into question? But the pursuit of the individual is merely one purpose of this journey. For, in investigating deviance, we encounter normative discourses aimed at either limiting or facilitating diversity. By whom were such religious positions established? How were they implemented? Whatever individual religious activity there may have been, it took place within a social context where a degree of rigour prevailed, and where the other way was the norm. That the context itself varied makes our work no easier, but it does make it more interesting. It is not our aim to portray Roman religion as unchanging, but to historicize it.

This book rejects the position that sources received from antiquity, especially the normative, judgemental, and condemnatory texts, reveal only that other way, and provide access only to the exclusive and excluding polemic of an intellectual elite. My argument, echoing Michel de Certeau,[1] rests on the assumption that such texts also provide a view of the highly varied, distorted, hyperbolic, and "devious" ways in which such norms were appropriated by individuals, even if those individuals remain anonymous. In my concluding chapter, I seek to clarify how such individual modes of appropriation were in turn predicated upon particular historical circumstances. That the norms themselves were merely attempts to represent a complex reality that resisted being subjected to such formulations is shown by the often encountered reference to a close association of divination, divine "revelation" accessible to the individual, with deviance.

What is "religious deviance"? To achieve some distance from ancient terminology – which will of course have an important role to play – I refer to a textbook sociological definition of deviance:[2]

> Deviance is any activity perceived to infringe a generally valid norm of a society or of a particular group within that society. Thus deviance is not a phenomenon that is regarded merely as atypical or unusual ... In order for behaviour to be regarded as deviant, it must be judged to offend against binding, socially defined standards. And, as many such standards, but not others, are codified in statutes, the phenomenon of deviance includes criminal behaviour ... but also behaviour that, while not regarded as illegal, is generally seen as unethical, immoral, eccentric, indecent, or simply "unhealthy". (tr. D. Richardson)

Sources

But where are we to find such "unhealthy" individuals, and their self-styled physicians? Is it even possible to reconstruct a consistent discourse as to the limits of acceptable religious behaviour? First of all, we have normative texts of highly varying character. Instances of the regulation of religion in the form of statutes are rare. The incorporation of religion into the systematizing structure of law is a very long process.[3] It begins in Rome in the early third century BCE, with the introduction of the written calendar

---

[1] de Certeau 1988.
[2] Joas 2001, 170.
[3] Ando 2006.

in the form of the *fasti*, a term whose sense might be rendered as "list of appropriate days for opening legal proceedings".[4] From its emergence in discrete rules in respect of priesthoods and the politically highly relevant area of the auspices (a particular form of divination),[5] the development does not attain a fundamentally new level until the *De legibus* of Cicero (106–43 BCE), with its outline of a religious statute, the post-Republican[6] city statutes, and the Augustan age.[7] It is not, however, until the legal corpora of Late Antiquity that we find comprehensive rules with the power of law, in particular the norms of the fourth and fifth centuries assembled in Book 16 of the *Codex Theodosianus*.

It is not statutory form that characterizes those descriptions of religious practice that we categorize as "antiquarian". They include accounts of the augural system and the festivals of the Roman year, commentaries on traditional religious songs, and the comprehensive work on "antiquities of religion", where the universal scholar Varro (116–27 BCE), in giving a written account of what was seen at the time, in the mid-first century BCE, as traditional religion, systematizes[8] and normalizes the field, and occasionally anticipates deviance.

We have no crime statistics for Roman antiquity, and so descriptions are typically of an anecdotal character, concentrated on a few individual instances. When ancient historiographers mention the theme, it is often to write about scandals, instances of aberrant behaviour that possessed great resonance. These are the few surviving instances of actual behaviour assessed by third parties, and concern such individuals as the nobleman Gaius Valerius Flaccus, who did not want to be made a priest, more precisely *flamen Dialis*, and the consul Flamininus, who disregarded divine portents.[9] Then there are some works of social criticism and philosophy. It is hard to tell the extent to which the criteria they express were generally accepted. They nevertheless represent clear-cut positions in a discourse on deviance, as when the poet Juvenal makes fun of the Sabbath practices of Roman women. Only in very few instances do such texts take on a systematic character; I have in mind here the work *De superstitione* – usually translated as *On Superstition*, and surviving only in a few, nevertheless substantial fragments – by the Stoic philosopher,

[4] Rüpke 2011b, 45.
[5] Rüpke 2005a and 2011b.
[6] Here I follow the periodization proposed by Harriet Flower (2010).
[7] Ando in Ando and Rüpke 2006, 9.
[8] Rüpke 2009a.
[9] See Livy 27.8.4–10 resp. Cic. *Div.* 1.77 f.

tragedian, and statesman Lucius Annaeus Seneca (died in 65 CE). This
text will receive closer attention, as will its counterpart the treatise *Peri
deisidaimonia*, already cited and written only a little later by the Middle
Platonist Plutarch at the end of the first century CE.

Brief mention should be made here of the search for traces of deviant
behaviour in material relics, which is faced with great difficulties. Evidence
of votive gifts and votive inscriptions, and also tombstones and funerary
inscriptions, may well be present in great quantities; they may indicate
a further spectrum of variations and further lines of inquiry; those variations may even be, as stated in the definition already cited, "atypical
or unusual". But the critical element is missing: we almost never know
whether such exceptional cases were also, to quote the same definition,
"seen as unethical, immoral, eccentric, indecent, or simply 'unhealthy'".[10]

Once more, this leads us to the problem of norms. How do they
make their presence felt? In what field are they valid? In the context of
the above-mentioned field of dedications and gravestones, one might
speak of areas of practice whose norms were mainly defined by *mos*, or
custom and tradition. With Pierre Bourdieu,[11] we might here think of an
interplay between habit on the one hand and "ideal conceptions" on the
other: while "habit" might describe an entire complex of unconsciously
acquired dispositions comprising sequences of actions, physical postures,
and even emotions, "ideal conceptions" would involve the conscious
assumption of social rules as to "how things should be". Such shared conceptions do not simply describe "how things really are", but they nevertheless remain affected by that concern. Here we might ascribe a strong,
standardizing effect to the great resources devoted to "public ritual" (*sacra
publica*) and the ceremonies of the elite: one sees how such things should
be done. And such a norm is not undermined by the fact that concrete
circumstances, topographical considerations, financial means, or pressure
of time[12] might lead to substantial transgressions that would still fall short
of being classified as "deviance".

The areas affected by explicit normalization might be slight in comparison, despite the casuistic tradition of the existence since Numa of
so-called royal laws, the *leges regiae* regulating, for example, who had to
offer which sacrifice to which god if the enemy commander had perished
in single combat at the hand of a Roman. In these circumstances, the

---

[10] But compare the evidence analysed e.g. by Minoja 2006.
[11] See Bourdieu 1972, 1998.
[12] I have in mind the necessity for rapid burials.

question of who had the prerogative to formulate norms is particularly important, and I shall accordingly give it especial attention in my analysis of the texts. Explicit religious authority did not simply lie with the social elite, but received legitimation from specific institutions such as the Senate or priesthoods; it could also be put in question by the charismatic authority of *vates*.[13]

Superstitio

What research strategy is appropriate in view of this state of the evidence? Building on older studies,[14] Dale Martin and Richard Gordon have made important terminological and etymological investigations into a concept that is of central importance in the context of non-criminal religious deviance. *Superstitio* is normally translated as "superstition", and this in itself serves to make us aware of the weight of prejudice borne along by such a concept.

A New Testament scholar based at Yale, Martin concentrates on philosophical and medical discourse from Hellenism into Late Antiquity, and Christian reception of the term *superstitio*.[15] His central thesis is that a fundamental change in the thinking of the political and cultural elite occurred during the course of the Imperial age. The world picture typical of city-state republics can be summed up in terms of a fundamentally positive anthropology: all people should be good, and are capable of being so. This results in a positive picture of the cosmos and the gods: just as only the good person is happy, so the gods, who are *by definition* happy,[16] must be good. Only in reaction to the experience of the Imperial age (admittedly never mentioned in such precise terms by Martin) did doubts arise, extending to the elite, in respect of this "grand optimal illusion": among the gods too there is capriciousness and wickedness; apart from the gods, and enabling the gods to remain good, there are demons, of whom it is reasonable to be afraid.

The term "superstition" (the modern usage makes it easier to bring together the histories of both word and concept) should be understood against the background of an initial premise: if the gods are good, it is

---

[13] See Rüpke 2007b, 231. For an example from the third century BCE: North 2000.
[14] See, for instance, for Cicero, Störling 1894; Solmsen 1944; in general, Belardi 1976 and Smith and Knight 2008, in particular, the comparative introduction in Smith 2008.
[15] Martin 2004.
[16] This optimistic vision, for example in Plutarch, stemmed from Plato: Moellering 1963, 95.

unreasonable to fear them. The censure of behaviour as "superstitious", attested for the first time in Theophrastus in the fourth century BCE,[17] serves to support this positive theology. Fearful behaviour towards the gods indicates a false theology. This redefining of the concept of *deisidaimonia*, which had long been and still continued to be a positive concept, was made plausible by a ploy that turned socially defined decorum into a theological criterion:

> Theophrastus' rejection of many popular beliefs and practices as "superstitions" is at base a matter of ethics expressed as etiquette: superstitious beliefs are wrong because they cause people to act in ways that are socially inappropriate, embarrassing and vulgar.[18]

A mere glance at Theophrastus' text makes it abundantly clear that a superstitious person is not "normal": in an entirely pragmatic sense, he is hardly even capable of life. Such a concept, once established, can also be directed against Christians, who do not share that illusion of the optimal world:

> *Deisidaimonía*, I need hardly say, would seem to be a sort of cowardice with respect to the divine; and your *deisidaímon* such as will not sally forth for the day till he have washed his hands and sprinkled himself at the Nine Springs, and put a bit of bay leaf from a temple in his mouth. And, if a weasel cross his path, he will not proceed on his way till someone else be gone by, or he have cast three stones across the street (to break the curse). Should he espy a snake in his house, if it be one of the red sort he will call upon Sabazius, if of the sacred, build a shrine then and there. When he crosses one of the smooth stones set up at crossroads, he anoints it with oil from his flask, and will not go on his way till he have knelt down and worshipped it. If a mouse gnaw a bag of his meal, he will off to the diviner, and ask what he must do, and, if the answer be "send it to the cobbler's to be patched", he neglects the advice and frees himself of the ill by rites of aversion. He is for ever purifying his house on the plea that Hecate has been drawn thither. Should owls hoot when he is abroad, he is much put about, and will not be on his way till he have cried "Athena forfend!" Set foot on a tomb he will not, nor come nigh a dead body nor a woman in childbed; he must keep himself unpolluted. On the fourth and twenty-fourth days of every month he has wine mulled for his household, and goes out to buy myrtle boughs, frankincense, and a holy picture, and then, returning, spends the livelong day doing sacrifice to the Hermaphrodites and putting garlands about them. He never has a dream but he flies to a diviner, or a soothsayer, or an interpreter of visions, to ask what god or goddess he

---

[17] Eitrem 1955, 166–7, refers to the portrayal of what may be a mourning ritual from the very early fourth century BCE, exceptionally depicting such a mode of behaviour.
[18] Martin 2004, 34.

should appease; and, when he is about to be initiated into the holy orders of Orpheus, he visits the priests every month and his wife with him, or, if she have not the time, the nurse and children. He would seem to be one of those who are for ever going to the seaside to besprinkle themselves; and, if ever he see one of the figures of Hecate at the crossroads wreathed with garlic, he is off home to wash his head and summon priestesses, whom he bids purify him with the carrying about him of a sea onion or a puppy-dog. If he catch sight of a madman or an epileptic, he shudders and spits in his bosom. (Theophrastus, *Characters* 16; tr. based on J. M. Edmonds, London, Heinemann, 1929)

Richard Gordon, a specialist in ancient religions based at Erfurt University, has paid particular regard to the Latin etymology, holding the philosophical discourse and its theological content as examined by Martin to be less important; instead, entirely in the sense of Émile Durkheim's comprehensive assessment of the positive aspects of deviance, he has concentrated on the further content and functions of that discourse. For Martin, the Greek theological discourse on *superstitio* trails centuries behind political events. Gordon, on the other hand, holds the Latin discourse of the senatorial elite to be an instrument forged in the white heat of political developments, serving to marginalize groups regarded as problematic.[19]

Gordon and Martin nevertheless share one fundamental observation. The behaviour branded – after Plautus[20] – as *superstitio* is improper and inappropriate, not technically false or ineffective. We accordingly find as antonyms such diverse terms as *religio* and, although rarely, *pietas*.[21] Two fields of application can be discerned: essentially unnecessary fears of divine anger, and foreign religions. Both fields indicate an elite using the term to differentiate its own religion, which was highly important for political communication and the assertion of hegemony. It was this motivating principle – the presumption of judgement over others, the assertion of belonging, and the perceived need for sharp differentiation – that defined the effectiveness of the term's use, rather than any particular force inherent to it.[22] In this "soft" form, the term fulfilled an important bridging function, and an integrative role: it was able to articulate the real tension that existed between the religion of the elite, calculated, in its public form, to legitimate the expansion of hegemony, and the

[19] Gordon 2008, 74; for the critique of Martin, see Gordon 2006.
[20] See Belardi 1976, 31–4 and Hoffmann 1985–8, who demonstrate the generally positive associations of the concept in the sense of "prophecy".
[21] Gordon 2008, 79–80. For the very limited importance of *pietas* in the field of religious practices, see Schröder 2012. For the antonymic character of *religio*, see De Souza 2011.
[22] Gordon 2008, 81–6, 76–7.

religion of the general populace, with its function of managing the contingencies of everyday life.[23]

Gordon also registers an important break that occurred during the Imperial age, coinciding with the recentring of religion on the ruler cult and the associated cult of Jupiter Optimus Maximus, the supreme deity of the Roman polity. This cult complex developed considerable integrative power, going so far as to embrace the population's need for religious succour in personal crises: an instance of an interest in the instrumental aspect of religion. In this way, the polemical content of *superstitio* could be concentrated on foreign religions, which could readily be associated with stereotypes such as feminine, emotional, credulous, and barbaric: the Jews provided a good example.[24] With the extension of Roman citizenship to the entire Roman Empire, the Empire's self-definition in terms of a commonality that was essentially merely imagined acquired a new degree of vagueness, which allowed it to elide with *humanitas*, while at the same time consigning opposing internal models of group identification to full illegitimacy. Now, in the third and fourth centuries, *superstitio* became coincident with magic and treacherous divination.[25] To a corresponding degree, the expression entered legal texts and became a weapon that could be employed both against and by Christianity. As such it characterizes our late sources.

Religious deviance

At this point in the state of research, what questions remain to be answered? In a brief, peripheral remark, Gordon points to an important circumstance: by no means is the entire spectrum of ancient discourse on religious deviance covered by the term *superstitio*. This is true of the extreme forms of religious deviance mentioned by Gordon, which incurred the death penalty. But it also applies to those forms of aberrant behaviour, beginning with far smaller ritual errors, discussed in 1981 in a book, edited by John Scheid, on "religious crimes". Scheid further develops the theme[26] in his book on religion and piety.[27] Here, he is interested in the religious character and religious classification of misdemeanours,

[23] Gordon 2008, 89.
[24] More generally, Lieu, North, and Rajak 1994; Schäfer 1997; Horbury 1998; Janowitz 2001. For the later period, see Yuval, Harshav, and Chipman 2008.
[25] Gordon 2008, 93.
[26] Scheid 1981.
[27] Scheid 1985, 2nd edn 2001.

including those that were covered by the term *crimen*. He is able to demonstrate that, in this internal discourse, instances of deviance were always constructed as a burden on the community. An emphasis was thus placed on rituals, incumbent on the community, designed to relieve that burden and restore the *pax deorum*, or harmonious understanding with the gods: "the necessity for religious mediation by the whole of society".[28] Criminalization of the individual was largely absent. Here, the question of the grounds for, and possible expressive value of, such instances of aberrant behaviour remains open. The political and military contexts in which they occur suggest that it was in these particular areas, and probably not in the religious domain, that the motivation for individual instances lay.

This leads us to the second area that remains open to inquiry: both Martin and Gordon point to the discrepancy between the standards of the elite and the religious practices of others. In the context of an inquiry into individualism, this discrepancy in itself gives sufficient cause to investigate the practices that were subjected to such criticism. It is perhaps at this very point – and here too we may refer to Durkheim – that we should investigate the productivity of such deviant practices, and, with regard to the history of religion, the dynamic they released. It is not, or at least not merely, the positions taken up by political and religious leadership groups that should be weighed as important factors in religious-historical developments; changes in religious practices among the populace at large are also relevant.

It follows that, in pursuing a sociological and criminological investigation of deviance, we should not inquire solely on constructivist lines into processes such as labelling, exclusion and the creation of otherness, regulation and the construction of deviance.[29] It is my intention in this volume to use deviance as a means of approaching the question of individualization, and to inquire on an "objectivist" (or positivist) basis into the forms of and grounds for aberrant behaviour, while accepting the norm as a given.[30] My justification in so doing does not lie in an "absolutist" assumption that particular forms of religious activity can be classified as deviant regardless of the contexts within which the judgements in question were made, as does the article on *Aberglaube* in the Pauly-Wissowa *Realencyclopädie* (covering sixty-five columns) or the *Handwörterbuch des*

---

[28] Scheid 1981, 166. *Pax*: 167.
[29] *Relativist* or *reactivist* theories of deviant behaviour: see Perrin 2001; Thio, Calhoun, and Conyers 2008, 3.
[30] See Thio, Calhoun, and Conyers 2008, 3.

deutschen Aberglaubens (in ten volumes). To reiterate, my purpose is rather to obtain some idea of the breadth of individual religious activity and positions espoused by minorities, or marginalized by the dominance of the elite literary tradition, and, following Certeau,[31] to peruse normative texts for indications of transgressive individual attitudes. For the creation of norms can also always be seen as an attempt to control diversity.

These are the considerations that form the background to the remaining chapters of this volume. In a first step (Chapter 2), I will investigate normative texts from the Roman Republic for explicit statements and implicit indications regarding religious deviance, in respect of both their semantics and the content of the behaviour they designate as deviant. In so doing, and with the current state of research in mind, I will initially concentrate on legal and antiquarian fragments, taking my test material from the ancient collection of fragments of Roman jurists prior to the legal corpora of the emperor Justinian (*Iurisprudentia anteiustiniana*: there is still no more recent collection of these texts), and the two great *summae*, Varro's *Antiquitates rerum divinarum*, which we sadly have only in highly fragmentary form, and Cicero's *Laws*. In the third and fourth chapters I will turn to the first century CE, first to an interesting view on a concept of religious deviance as being due to lack of knowledge, developed by Valerius Maximus in the Tiberian age (Chapter 3). In Chapter 4, I will address the works of Seneca and Plutarch already mentioned. Here I will focus on one central – and surprising – phenomenon, which serves particularly to clarify the interplay between the public religious infrastructure and individual action; that is to say, behaviour in temples. For my third step I will proceed to later periods of the Imperial age, returning to legal texts and in particular the texts of statutes up to the period of Late Antiquity (Chapter 5). Finally, I will review ancient conceptualizations of the importance of individual religious experiences and decisions (Chapter 6), and will summarize my findings in a model of religious developments within the Imperial age (Chapter 7).

---

[31] Certeau 2007 (where he is generalizing observations of Certeau 1988).

CHAPTER 2

Creation of religious norms in the late Republic

Early prohibitions

The collection *Iurisprudentia anteiustiniana*, whose first edition was produced by P. E. Huschke in 1860, is concerned with legal texts. While our knowledge of these extends back to quotations in authors from the first century BCE (Cicero, Varro), in many instances we have to rely on texts from the Imperial age (Pliny, Gellius, Festus, Censorinus, Nonius) and even Late Antiquity (Servius, Macrobius). It is often interest in particularly ancient institutions, rare words, or contemporary survivals that has given rise to a particular quotation. Although the texts available to us are not representative, inevitable distortions of the tradition can be tolerated insofar as they are unconnected with my interest in the material.

The very first fragment in the collection is relevant. It is ascribed to the *pontifex maximus* who was the first to set up a placard displaying "legal topics" in front of his official premises (*consulere licet*). Ti. Coruncanius[1] decrees in the early third century BCE that "Ruminants cannot be clean animals for sacrifice until they have two permanent teeth" (*Coruncanius ruminalis hostias, donec bidentes fierent, puras negauit*).[2] Evidently, the pontiff is intervening against a practice of attempting to reduce the cost of certain sacrifices by using very young animals. As is always the case in respect of normative texts, it is difficult to assess the extent of the particular behaviour now defined as a violation.

The pontiff Ser. Fabius Pictor, in the first half of the second century BCE,[3] wrote exhaustively about pontifical law in his work *De iure pontificio*. The title is confirmed by two independent users, Gellius and Nonius, which shows that, already a hundred years before Cicero, *ius* had become

---

[1] Rüpke 2008 (in the following *FS* = *Fasti sacerdotum*), No. 1399, *Pontifex maximus c.* 254–243 BCE.
[2] *Iur.* 1.
[3] *FS* 1600.

an attractive formula for systematizing ritual knowledge.[4] Gellius in the second century CE, in the *Attic Nights*, his twenty-volume collection of erudition for dinner-table conversation, cites from Pictor a substantial passage on ritual norms (*caerimoniae*) imposed on the *flamen Dialis*, the priest of Jupiter. The language of the prohibitions is colourful: *religio est, fas numquam est, fas non est, ius non est, piaculum est, neque tangere ... mos est, neque ... fas est, licitum non est, fas non est, ius non est*, concluding with *tamen ... non est religio* ("it is questionable, it is never permitted, it is not permitted, it is not legally valid, it is a ritual violation, it is neither tradition nor permitted, it is not allowed, (again) not legally valid", and "nevertheless ... it is not pious").[5] It is impossible to find correlations with the various terms chosen either in the subjects of the rules – from riding to remarriage – or in the strictness of the prohibitions. An exception is the prohibition denoted *piaculum*, which affected third parties, and applied only for the remainder of the day in question.[6] This represents a "soft" norm, whose infringement affected the rights of third parties, and might be ritually expiated: the *flamen Dialis* offered a kind of asylum to a person condemned to be flogged, postponing the punishment for one day. The wording of Fabius' text is not certain: Gellius announces a paraphrase with the words *unde haec ferme sunt ...*; but there is no apparent reason why the later compiler should have chosen a strong linguistic variant here. It appears to have been Sergius Fabius Pictor himself who played freely with traditional terms in the systematization he characterized as *ius*: the terminology does not conform with later theory, which assigned *fas* to the religious sphere, *ius* to the profane.[7]

For the second half of the second century BCE, Cicero ascribes positions taken in respect of inheritance law[8] to the pontiff Publius Mucius Scaevola.[9] At issue was the question as to how small the shares in an inheritance had to be in order to obviate the duty to perpetuate the family cults, which would otherwise fall upon all the heirs equally. Cicero here exploits an unattractive mixture of pontifical law and civil law. Fragment 4 by the same author concerns the cult of the dead, namely the effect on the family's normal burial rituals if the corpse remained at sea, whether through being drowned or having been killed previously. Here, ritual

---

[4] Cf. Ando 2006, 135 for the first century.
[5] *Iur.* 3 = Gell. *NA* 10.15.1–30.
[6] On the concept of *piaculum* see Scheid 1985, 35–6; Rüpke 1995, 258–61; Rüpke 2011b, 50–2.
[7] Thus Serv. *Georg.* 1.269.
[8] *Iur.* 3 = Cic. *Leg.* 2. 52–3.
[9] *FS* 2476. Scaevola died between 121 and 115 BCE.

cleanliness (*purus*) was achieved after the performance of minimal rites, as the deceased, or his finger bone severed at the time of cremation, did not remain unburied and thus in a disquieting status. The fifth fragment, also from Cicero, relays a *responsum* of the pontifical college in 123 BCE: in the absence of a decision of the people, the dedication of a plot of land by the Vestal Licinia[10] remained invalid, failing to give the action the quality of *sacer*. This ruling also concerned the duties and obligations of third parties, limiting the options open to the sole heir but also having the effect of affirming the continuity of ritual procedures.

The cousin of the same Scaevola, Q. Mucius P. f. Scaevola,[11] wrote eighteen volumes of civil law, although those of his remarks on religion-related subjects that are cited at a later date cannot be assigned to this work with any certainty. His distinction between the intentional (*prudens*) and non-intentional (*imprudens*) infringement of rules relating to feast days was groundbreaking: only in the latter instance was expiation possible by *piaculum*.[12] Also regarding feast days, he developed the formula that those things were allowed that would cause harm if left undone, so preventing the day from being defiled (*polluisse*).[13] Cicero developed his own conception of religious law in contention with the requirement of this same Scaevola that a good pontiff should distinguish himself by his knowledge of civil law.[14]

To summarize so far: the many fragments from authors of the third to early first centuries include very few rules regarding religion. This confirms views of the fundamental "secularity" of Roman law, whose power lay precisely in the area of opening up spaces for argument that remained free of the claims of new and old gods that might otherwise be asserted case by case.[15] At the same time, this law long dominated by the priesthood of the pontiffs displayed extreme caution when it came to regulating the realm characterized by claims of the gods. The religious element is missing even from the Twelve Tables, which we begin to discern only in the commentaries and handbooks of this same epoch. At most, rules for cremation and burial regulating locality, social roles, and the degree of luxury of graves may be assigned to this category on functional grounds (in the tenth Table); the semantics in themselves suggest nothing of the

---

[10] *FS* 2218; she was executed in 113 BCE.
[11] *FS* 2478; died in 82 BCE.
[12] *Iur.* 10 and 11.
[13] *Iur.* 12.
[14] *Iur.* 14 = Cic. *Leg.* 2.47.
[15] See Tellegen-Couperus 2012.

kind. The prohibition on "charming" crops by means of song[16] appears to belong in a criminal law context. This prompts an inquiry into the whys and wherefores of other rules regarding religion.

To a striking degree, the few fragments concerned with religion involve the roles of the *sacerdotes publici*, the public religion specialists; even the problem of the sacral quality of plots of land (*sacer*) is discussed in such contexts. This chimes with the "anecdotal" evidence of historiographical texts, a great number of which involve such cases of deviance and role conflict.[17]

In these instances, however, the terminology of the rules that have come down to us is distinctly legalistic. The same applies to inheritance law insofar as it concerned the continuity of family cults.[18] The evidently substantial interest of testators in such an obligation conflicted with the disinterest of heirs, providing the occasion for extensive argumentation by civil lawyers. This very conflict was the subject of comment by Cicero.

In addition to the instances mentioned so far, we find others that are characterized by the terminology of purity and defilement. Deviance here appears to be a problem of deficient ritual knowledge or insufficient information in particular situations. Intent must be discounted. The ritual apparatus preserves its meaning by the use of ritual devices to remedy ritual errors: *piaculum* is a virtual panacea against religious deviance. It is scarcely an accident that feast days are a theme: copies of the *fasti* calendar, a genre that combined religious and legal information in published form, were increasingly available.[19] Fundamental alternatives to a religious system that is itself the subject of constant implicit reference are not addressed here. It is the system in place that demands elaboration.

The *Senatusconsultum de Bacchanalibus*, the 186 BCE Senate resolution concerning the cults of Dionysus,[20] provides a unique contemporary control text.

> (1) [Q(uintus)] Marcius L(uci) f(ilius), S(purius) Postumius L(uci) f(ilius) co(n)s(ules) senatum consoluerunt n(onis) Octob(ribus), apud aedem (2) Duelonai. Sc(ribundo) arf(uerunt) M(arcus) Claudi(us) M(arci) f(ilius), L(ucius) Valeri(us) P(ubli) f(ilius), Q(uintus) Minuci(us) C(ai) f(ilius). De Bacanalibus quei foiderati (3) esent, ita exdeicendum censuere:

[16] Plin. *HN* 28.10–17.
[17] See Rüpke 2010b.
[18] For the underlying social mechanisms cf. Mouritsen 1997 on Pompeii.
[19] Comprehensively discussed in Rüpke 1995; also 2011a, in condensed English translation.
[20] *CIL* I².581 = *ILLRP* 511.

Neiquis eorum [B]acanal habuise velet. seiques (4) esent, quei sibei deicerent necesus ese Bacanal habere, eeis utei ad pr(aitorem) urbanum (5) Romam venirent, deque eeis rebus, ubei eorum v[e]r[b]a audita esent, utei senatus (6) noster decerneret, dum ne minus senator[i]bus C adesent, [quom e]a res cosoleretur.

(7) Bacas vir nequis adiese velet ceivis Romanus neve nominus Latini neve socium (8) quisquam, nisei pr(aitorem) urbanum adiesent, isque [d]e senatuos sententiad, dum ne (9) minus senatoribus C adesent, quom ea res cosoleretur, iousisent. Ce[n]suere.

(10) sacerdos nequis uir eset. Magister neque uir neque mulier quisquam eset. (11) neve pecuniam quisquam eorum comoine[m h]abuise velet. Neve magistratum, (12) neve pro magistratu[d], neque virum [neque mul]ierem qui[s]quam fecise velet. (13) Neve post hac inter sed conioura[se nev]e comvovise neve conspondise (14) neve conpromesise velet, neve quisquam fidem inter sed dedise velet.

(15) Sacra in [o]quoltod ne quisquam fecise velet. Neve in poplicod neve in (16) preivatod neve exstrad urbem sacra quisquam fecise velet, nisei (17) pr(aitorem) urbanum adieset, isque de senatuos sententiad, dum ne minus (18) senatoribus C adesent, quom ea res cosoleretur, iousisent. Censuere.

(19) Homines plous V oinvorsei virei atque mulieres sacra ne quisquam (20) fecise velet, neve inter ibei virei plous duobus, mulieribus plous tribus (21) arfuise velent, nisei de pr(aitoris) urbani senatuosque sententiad, utei suprad (22) scriptum est.

The consuls Quintus Marcius, son of Lucius, and Spurius Postumius, son of Lucius, consulted with the Senate on the Nones (7) of October at the temple of Bellona.

Responsible for the minutes were the signatories Marcus Claudius son of Marcus, Lucius Valerius son of Publius, and Quintus Minucius son of Gaius.

They decided, concerning the Bacchanalia, that the confederates are to announce as follows:

None of them shall seek to hold (a place for) Bacchanalia; if there are those who think it necessary for them to hold a Bacchanal, they will go to the urban praetor in Rome, and, as soon as their petition has been heard, our Senate will decide on these matters, provided that no fewer than one hundred senators are present to consult upon the matter.

No man shall seek to frequent (female) bacchantes, neither a Roman citizen nor a Latin nor one of the allies, unless he go to the urban praetor, and the urban praetor order it on the basis of a decision of the Senate, with no less than one hundred senators being present when the matter is consulted upon. They decided.

No man shall be a priest; no magistrate or any man, nor any woman. And none of them shall seek to have a common treasury, and no one seek to make a man or a woman a magistrate or promagistrate (in the association).

And no one shall seek in the future to group together by means of an oath or vow, a compact or a promise, and no one shall seek to give a promise of loyalty to another. No one shall seek to perform a ritual in secret. No one shall seek to perform a ritual in public or in private or outside the city, unless they go to the city praetor and he order it on the basis of a decision of the Senate, with no less than one hundred senators being present when the matter is consulted upon. They decided.

No one shall seek that more than five people, men and women together, perform a ritual, or seek that more than two men and more than three women be among that number, unless it be by a decision of the urban praetor and the Senate, as written above. (*There follow closing stipulations designed to ensure wide publication and circulation of the decision*; tr. D. Richardson/J. Rüpke)

Here in precise terms, a particular type of rite or ritual location, together with a group structure, is prohibited or placed under strict supervision. The resolution mentions neither the god Dionysus, Bacchus, nor Liber Pater, nor unfitting or incorrect behaviour during the rite. Instead, a senior rank within the organizational structure is merely forbidden. The cult is forbidden to carry out activities "in secret". "In public", "in private", and "outside the city" are alternatives that require approval. It is the outlined procedure itself that ends the secrecy of the rite. While the effect may have been a broad prohibition, and was even perhaps so intended, this is not stated in so many words.

Varro

Both Varro's *Antiquitates rerum humanarum et divinarum* and Cicero's *De legibus* fall within the first period that can no longer be understood as part of the Roman Republic.[21] While the *Laws* still belong to the fifties, the *Antiquitates* of Cicero's older contemporary may have been written only shortly before Caesar's death, and published in 47 BCE. In the barely 300 fragments of the sixteen books *De rebus divinis*, religious deviance is evoked rather than described in concrete terms. The work's didactic intention suggests that Varro sees the cause of deviant behaviour in defective knowledge. This should be noted as we go through the text, and it is immediately evident in the earliest fragments, where Varro refers to his books as remedies against "neglect by the citizens" and obscurity.[22]

---

[21] Flower 2010.
[22] Frr. 2a and 2b Cardauns. In individual cases, the sequence of the fragments in Cardauns is disputable; but it is on the whole well-founded. See Rüpke 2014c for the thrust of Varro's argument about (historical) knowledge.

Only in a few instances does Varro report on historical cases, and add assessments of his own. Fragment 93 (Book 14) refers to the development of a cult of Liber by women who proceeded to celebrate Bacchanalia "with extreme frenzy", and reports the subsequent displeasure of the Senate (*senatui displicuerunt*). The connection with the case in 186 BCE, described above, is self-evident. Varro talks of Liber again and in more detail in Book 16 (*On Selected Gods*), where he refers to a cult of Liber in neighbouring Lavinium. In the context of a procession with a phallus, the worthiest matron had to set a garland on the unworthy member,[23] in a ritual that was presumably still practised in Varro's lifetime, thus after the resolution of 186.[24] This throws new light on the reference in fragment 45 to the effect that the cult of Liber Pater had been eliminated from the whole of Italy by resolution of the Senate.

In Book 8 on feast days, fragment 78 talks of ritual problems in the approach to earthquakes. Here, the suggestion is that the ancient Romans avoided naming the deity who had caused the earthquake. This was so that "the people would not be bound by a false *religio*" because of a confusion of names. When feast days had been defiled by someone, the expiation (*piaculo*) was addressed to an unspecified deity (*si deo si deae*). The same form of deviant behaviour is treated in fragment 79: it is against *religio* to water the fields or wash animals on feast days, as "the nymphs cannot be moved without *piaculum*". Evidently, both subject and terminology follow the model of the older juridical texts treated above.[25]

The remaining relevant fragments are probably from Book 1. An old topic – and evidently the source of repeated instances of deviance – is the dedication of temples without a senatorial resolution (fr. 44). Fragment 46 relates a contemporary (59 BCE) dispute over the establishment of a cult of four Egyptian gods on the Capitol.

> Serapem et Isidem et Arpocratem et Anubem prohibitos Capitolio (Varro commemorat) eorumque <aras> a senatu deiectas nonnisi per uim popularium restructas.

> Varro recorded that Serapis, Isis, Harpocrates, and Anubis were banned from the Capitol; their altars were removed, and restored only by direct action of the people. (tr. J. Rüpke)

---

[23] Fr. 262: *membro inhonesto matrem familias honestissimam …*
[24] Augustine's text has no reference to this chronology of events.
[25] The terms *puritia* and *polluta* in fr. 48 cannot, effectively, be more precisely assigned; a ritual context is to be assumed (see Cardauns comm. ad loc).

Here, it appears that the opposing parties were the consuls and the Senate
on the one hand, and the people on the other. The account refrains from
any use of religious terminology. The to and fro of destruction and restoration is formulated solely in terms of power; in any event, the successful
performance of the sacrifice coincides with the suspension of the conflict
between consuls and people: a conflict escalated by consul Gabinius only
when compelled by the Senate.[26]

Varro too is familiar with the semantics of *religiosus* and *superstitiosus*.
The latter fears the gods; the former honours them (as he does his parents); this is indicated in fragment 47:[27]

> Cum religiosum a superstitioso ea distinctione discernat, ut a superstitioso
> (dicat) timeri deos, a religioso autem tantum uereri ut parentes, non ut
> hostes timeri, atque omnes ita bonos (dicat), ut facilius sit eos nocentibus
> parcere quam laedere quemquam innocentem …

> He differentiated the religious man from the superstitious in that the gods
> are feared by the superstitious, but by the religious man only venerated like
> his parents and not feared like enemies. And all the gods are good, so that it
> is easier for them to spare wrongdoers than to violate any innocent person.
> (tr. J. Rüpke)

Here Varro reflects philosophical discourse since Theophrastus. But he
fails to draw the same conclusions. Unlike Plutarch subsequently, in case
of doubt Varro opts for too much cult rather than too little.[28] Varro is
moved by the cult of images to complain that figurative representations of
the gods have removed fear of the gods, and led to error.[29] This critical attitude to images has an interesting consequence. Evidently distancing himself from other positions taken on the subject, Varro affirms that neglect
of images in the cult cannot lead to guilt (*culpa*).[30] This minority religious
position casts doubt on Varro's other judgements regarding deviance.

Varro's "three kinds of theology" (*tria genera theologiae*) has been written about often enough. I myself have taken the position that the aim of
this theory originated by Varro was not a distanced systematization, but a

---

[26] Fr. 46a.

[27] There is no indication in the tradition of a connection with fr. 46.

[28] Fr. 12: … *potius eos magis colere quam despicere vulgus velit* …

[29] Fr. 18: … *metum dempsisse et errorem addidisse* …

[30] Fr. 22: *Dii ueri neque desiderant ea (sc. sacra) neque deposcunt, ex aere autem facti, testa, gypso uel marmore multo minus haec curant; carent enim sensu; neque ulla contrahitur, si ea non feceris, culpa, neque ulla, si feceris, gratia* – "True gods neither wish nor demand such rituals; those made of bronze, clay, plaster, or marble care even less for they have no perception. There is no fault if you do not perform, nor any gratitude if you do perform them."

re-evaluation of actual religious practice in Rome, and the raising of the status of descriptions of that practice to the rank of philosophical theory.[31] In discussions of the question, sufficient account has not been taken of the normative character of Varro's description of the "theology of poets" (*genus mythicon*). Poetic representations of the gods "offend against the dignity and nature of the immortals".[32] This is a widespread instance of deviance, and one that is enjoyed on a massive scale. In face of it, Varro can only demand that it be at least spatially confined, and restricted to the theatre.[33] As I have stressed elsewhere, it was precisely this "theology" characterized as deviant that enjoyed the widest dissemination and offered the greatest potential for religious innovation.[34]

There was another form of deviance related to the theatre. In stage mimes, asking for water from the god of wine and wine from the *Lymphae* was a comedic device.[35] But Varro's reason for citing it is that he suspects the emergence of such a form of religious aberration on a mass scale due to uncertainty. It is this perceived danger that he is addressing.

Varro himself gives the *raison d'être* for his books as the deviant behaviour that he both observes and, to a greater extent, assumes to exist. Even if it had been possible, by going back to first principles, to conceive of a religion that was essentially clearer, and limited to only a few gods that could be justified philosophically, the fact remained that religion as it had developed over the course of history, and become institutionalized in Rome, relied on a highly complex apparatus of deities, and institutions that were specifically geared to it. The important thing was that the apparatus should operate correctly, and it was to this end that Varro wrote his

---

[31] Rüpke 2005a.
[32] Fr. 7: ... *Primum ... quod dixi, in eo sunt multa contra dignitatem et naturam inmortalium ficta. In hoc enim est, ut deus alius ex capite, alius ex femore sit, alius ex guttis sanguinis natus; in hoc ut dii furati sint, ut adulterarint, ut seruierint homini; denique in hoc omnia diis attribuuntur, quae non modo in hominem, sed etiam quae in contemptissimum hominem cadere possunt.* – "First, as I have said, there is a lot of fiction contrarious to the dignity and nature of the gods. Among which it has to be counted that a god is born out of a head, another out of the thigh, another out of drops of blood. Also that gods are thieves, adulterers, servants of a man. Finally, in (that type of text) all those events are attributed to gods that could happen not only to humankind, but even to the most vile of humans."
[33] Fr. 10.
[34] Rüpke 2006a, 125.
[35] Fr. 3: ... *ita esse utilem cognitionem deorum, si sciatur quam quisque deus uim et facultatem ac potestatem cuiusque causa deum inuocare atque aduocare debeamus, ne faciamus, ut mimi solent, et potemus a Libero aquam, a Lymphis uinum* – "... thus the knowledge of the gods would be useful, if it is known which power, potential, and realm every god has and for which reason we have to implore and call for the god, in order not to do as the mimes, that is to drink water from Liber (i.e. the god of wine) and wine from the Lymphs (i.e. the goddesses of water)."

sixteen books. Once again, it is no accident that, although Varro identifies the citizenry as a whole[36] as the target of his work, the first books after the introduction are aimed at the religious specialists charged with the apparatus, the *sacerdotes publici*. It was these (usually) senators who bore responsibility for the institutions. It was the Senate who held and applied regulatory power in the event of conflict, and it was this regulatory core whose functioning it was Varro's purpose to secure.

And the external limits? The "his (fellow) citizens" of Augustine's text in fragment 3 represents an illocutionary first-person "we". Occasionally, boundaries are indicated between this "we" and the *vulgus*, the common people; but the distinction between *populus* and Senate tends to be left to the bird's-eye perspective of the historical observer. These internal boundaries are unclear and mobile, temporary and contingent. The external limits remain implicit: they coincide with the limits of the city – the case of Lavinium! – or of the human group, the *cives*. This "we" is not endangered by isolated instances of deviancy. Theological exculpation, ritual expiation, or spatial delimitation are normally sufficient precaution and remedy. But deviancy on a mass scale through ignorance endangers the whole system. And religion in the mid-first century BCE had become a knowledge-based system, with all the dangers that this implied.

Cicero

It was in the 50s BCE, in Book 2 of *De legibus*, that Cicero turned a penetrating gaze on religion. He had evidently intended the text as an addition to his six books *De re publica*, published in May 51, shortly before his period of office as governor of Cilicia; "On Laws" was probably written during the same period, but remained unpublished.[37] The entire second book, and so the first series of positive stipulations, is devoted to religion.[38] Then, in Book 3, Marcus, the chief participant in the dialogue, addresses questions of power and legitimate rule, in the form not only of offices and procedures, but also of legislation. It is vital to note the pronounced parallels between the legislation in books 2 and 3. Thus in Book 2 Cicero opens his discussion (2.15):

> Sit igitur hoc iam a principio persuasum civibus, dominos esse omnium rerum ac moderatores deos, eaque quae gerantur eorum geri iudicio ac

---

[36] Fr. 3: ... *praestare se civibus suis ...*

[37] For discussion of the dating see P. L. Schmidt 1969, 288–92, and the comprehensive treatment by Dyck 2004, 5–7 and 22–3.

[38] See in general Turpin 1986; Sauer 2007; Rüpke 2012a, 186–204.

numine, eosdemque optime de genere hominum mereri, et qualia quisque sit, quid agat, quid in se admittat, qua mente, qua pietate colat religiones, intueri, piorumque et impiorum habere rationem.

So the citizens should first of all be convinced of this, that the gods are lords and masters of everything; that what is done is done by their decision and authority; that they are, moreover, great benefactors of mankind and observe what kind of person everyone is – his actions and misdemeanours, his attitude and devotion to religious duties – and take note of the pious and the impious. (tr. Niall Rudd, Penguin, 1998)

This should be compared with the introductory passage in 3.2–5:[39]

MARCUS. Videtis igitur magistratus hanc esse vim, ut praesit prae- scribatque recta utilia et coniuncta cum legibus. Ut enim magistratibus leges, ita populo praesunt magistratus, vereque dici potest, magistratum legem esse loquentem, legem autem mutum magistratum. Nihil porro tam aptum est ius condicionemque naturae – quod quom dico, legem a me dici intellegi volo –, quam imperium, sine quo nec domus ulla nec civitas nec gens nec hominum universum genus stare, nec rerum natura omnis nec ipse mundus potest. Nam et hic deo paret, et huic oboedi- unt maria terraque, et hominum vita iussis supremae legis obtempertat. Atque ut ad haec citeriora veniam et notiora nobis: Omnes antiques gen- tes regibus quondam paruerunt. Quod genus imperii primumad homines iustissimos et sapientissimos deferebatur (ideque et in re publica nostra maxime valuit, quoad ei regalos potestas praefuit), deinde etiam deinceps posteris prodebatur, quod et in iis etiam, qui nunc placuit, non ii nemini, sed non semper uni parere voluerunt. Nos autem quoniam leges damus liberis populis, quaeque de optima re publica sentiremus, in sex libris ante diximus, accommodabimus hoc tempore leges ad illum, quem probamus, civitatis statum. Magistratibus igitur opus est, sine quorum prudentia ac diligentia esse civitas non potest, quorumque discriptione omnis rei publi- cae moderatio continetur. Neque solum iis praescribendus est imperandi, sed etiam civibus obtemperandi modus. Nam et qui bene imperat, paru- erit aliquando necesse est, et qui modeste paret, videtur qui aliquando imperet dignus esse. Itaque oportet et eum qui paret sperare, se aliquo tempore imperaturum, et illum qui imperat cogitare, brevi tempore sibi esse parendum. Nec vero solum ut obtemperent oboediantque magistra- tibus, sed etiam ut eos colant diligantque praescribimus, ut Charondas in suis facit legibus. Noster vero Plato Titanum e genere statuit eos, qui illi caelestibus sic hi adversentur magistratibus. Quae cum ita sint, ad ipsas iam leges veniamus si placet.

ATTICUS: Mihi vero et istud et ordo iste rerum placet.

---

[39] Rüpke 2011a.

MARCUS: You appreciate, then, that a magistrate's function is to take charge and to issue directives which are right, beneficial, and in accordance with the laws. As magistrates are subject to the laws, the people are subject to the magistrates. In fact it is true to say that a magistrate is a speaking law, and law a silent magistrate. Nothing is so closely bound up with the decrees and terms of nature (and by that I wish to be understood as meaning law) as authority. Without that, no house or state or clan can survive – no, nor the human race, nor the whole of nature, nor the very universe itself. For the universe obeys God; land and sea abide by the laws of the universe; and human life is subject to the commands of the supreme law.

If I may come, now, to matters which are closer to us and more familiar – all ancient peoples were once subject to kings. That kind of power was originally vested in the wisest and the most just. (And that practice prevailed, for the most part, in our country as long as the kings reigned over it.) Subsequently that power was also entrusted to their descendants in succession, a custom which survives even in contemporary monarchies. Those who were opposed to monarchy wished to obey – not nobody, but not always a single person. However, here I am providing a body of law for free communities; so I will adjust my laws to the type of government which I think best. (In the six earlier books I presented my views about the best constitution.) Magistrates, then, are a necessity. Without their good sense and close attention there can be no state. In fact the whole management of a country depends on the apportionment of their functions. Not only must their authority be clearly delimited; the same applies also to the citizens' duty to obey them. A man who exercises power effectively will at some stage have to obey others, and one who quietly executes orders shows that he deserves, eventually, to wield power himself. So it must be the case that anyone who executes orders will have hopes of holding power at some time himself, while the man at present in charge will bear in mind that before long he will have to obey others. I lay it down, as Charondas does in his laws, that the people should not only obey the magistrates and carry out their instructions, but should also give them honour and esteem. Our friend Plato held that citizens who oppose the magistrates are descended from the Titans, who themselves opposed the gods. Having cleared the ground, let us now come to the laws themselves, if that's all right with you.

ATTICUS: Yes, it's all right with me, and so is the order in which you are treating the material. (tr. Niall Rudd, Penguin, 1998)

The existence and supremacy of the gods is as fundamental for "religion" as is the self-evidence of rule in the power structure of society.[40] Accordingly, in their deliberately archaic style, the opening sections of these texts

[40] For the central position of the gods see van den Bruwaene 1961.

themselves display a strict parallelism.[41] If higher powers are accepted as given, then the manner in which they are accessed suggests itself as a likely starting point. Other elements are less apparent, but explicable as arising from the intended parallelism. This is true as much for the punitive powers of the gods as for the presumption of obedience to magistrates. It is difficult to determine the extent of this principle of parallelism. A logic inherent to each theme, or associations of key concepts, could help to explain the sequence of the themes discussed. In any event, the unusual sequence at the beginning of the section on religion[42] can be better understood as an attempted parallelism. A discernible inner logic to the stipulations regarding magistrates begins with the principle of obedience and extends to the problem of contradiction and/or appeal (*provocatio*) and the distribution of powers between the magistrates (3.6), including the problem of command outside the confines of the city (*militiae*). Cicero's desire to establish a similar sequence for religion might explain why he introduces the problem of "separated gods" as early as the third sentence, and adds a stipulation for extra-urban sanctuaries, along with a classification of gods similar to his list of the various magistrates (2.19).

Conversely, the list of magistrates begins with those office-bearers with responsibilities for festivals and temples (these take pride of place in the field of possible activities: 3.7), thus adopting the structure of the stipulations for religion in respect of public festivals (*sollemnia* is a key term in both instances). This gives us the following as Cicero's text for religious rules (2.19–22):

> Ad diuos adeunto caste, pietatem adhibento, opes amouento. Qui secus faxit, deus ipse uindex erit.
>
> Separatim nemo habessit deos neue nouos neue aduenas nisi publice adscitos; priuatim colunto quos rite a patribus <acceperint. In urbibus> delubra habento. Lucos in agris habento et Larum sedes. Ritus familiae patrumque seruanto.
>
> Diuos et eos qui caelestes semper habiti sunt colunto et ollos quos endo caelo merita locauerint, Herculem, Liberum, Aesculapium, Castorem, Pollucem, Quirinum, ast olla propter quae datur homini ascensus in caelum, Mentem, Virtutem, Pietatem, Fidem, earumque laudum delubra sunto nec ulla uitiorum.
>
> Sacra sollemnia obeunto.

---

[41] Cf. 2.19 and 3.6. Again, this remains unrecognized in Dyck's commentary (2004, e.g. 240–3; 290–5; cf. 438–9 for discussion on the peculiarities of the structure of the laws in Book 3).

[42] As opposed to Dyck's assertion (2004, 242) that "the arrangement of the laws is fairly straightforward", a statement that cannot be supported.

Feriis iurgia <a>mouento, easque in famulis operibus patratis habento, itaque, ut ita cadat in annuis anfractibus, descriptum esto. Certasque fruges certasque bacas sacerdotes publice libanto, (20) hoc certis sacrificiis ac diebus. Itemque alios ad dies ubertatem lactis feturaeque seruanto, idque nec omitti possit, ad eam rem rationem, cursus annuos sacerdotes finiunto, quaeque quoique diuo decorae grataeque sint hostiae, prouidento.

Diuisque aliis <alii> sacerdotes, omnibus pontifices, singulis flamines sunto. Virginesque Vestales in urbe custodiunto ignem foci publici sempiternum.

Quoque haec et priuatim et publice modo rituque fiant, discunto ignari a publicis sacerdotibus. Eorum autem genera sunto tria: unum quod praesit caerimoniis et sacris, alterum quod interpretetur fatidicorum et uatium effata incognita, quorum senatus populusque adsciuerit. Interpretes autem Iouis optumi maxumi, publici augures, signis et auspiciis postera uidento, (21) disciplinam tenento sacerdotesque[43] uineta uirgetaque et salutem populi auguranto; quique agent rem duelli quique popularem, auspicium praemonento ollique obtemperanto. Diuorumque iras prouidento sisque apparento, caelique fulgura regionibus ratis temperanto, urbemque et agros et templa liberata et effata habento. Quaeque augur iniusta nefasta uitiosa dira deixerit, inrita infectaque sunto; quique non paruerit, capital esto.

Foederum pacis belli indotiarum ratorum fetiales iudices non<tii> sunto, bella disceptanto.

Prodigia portenta ad Etruscos [et] haruspices, si senatus iussit, deferunto, Etruriaque principes disciplinam doceto. Quibus diuis creuerint, procuranto, idemque fulgura atque obstita pianto.

Nocturna mulierum sacrificia ne sunto praeter olla quae pro populo rite fient. Neue quem ini<ti>anto nisi, ut adsolet, Cereri Graeco sacro.

(22) Sacrum commissum, quod neque expiari poterit, impie commissum, est<o>; quod expiari poterit, publici sacerdotes expianto.

Loedis publicis …, quod sine curriculo et sine certatione corporum fiat, popularem laetitiam in cantu et fidibus et tibiis moderanto eamque cum diuom honore iungunto.

Ex patriis ritibus optuma colunto.

Praeter Idaeae Matris famulos eosque iustis diebus ne quis stipem cogito.

Sacrum sacroue commendatum qui clepserit rapsitue, parricida esto.

Periurii poena diuina exitium, humana dedecus <esto>.

Incestum pontifices supremo supplicio sanciunto.

Impius ne audeto placare donis iram deorum.

Caute uota reddunto.

Poena uiolati iuris esto.

[Quocirca] Nequis agrum consecrato. Auri argenti eboris sacrandi modus esto.

---

[43] I do not follow the suggestion of Dyck (2004, 305) to delete *sacerdotes*, as the augurs have a specific interest to define the collaboration and the division of labour with the magistrates.

Sacra priuata perpetua manento.

Deorum Manium iura sancta sunto. <Bo>nos leto datos diuos habento. Sumptum in ollos luctumque minuunto.

No one shall have gods of his own, whether new or foreign, unless they have been officially brought in. In private they shall worship those gods whose worship has been handed down in its proper form by their forefathers.

In the cities they shall have shrines; in the countryside they shall have groves and abodes for their tutelary gods.

They shall preserve the rituals of their family and fathers.

They shall worship as gods those who have always been considered divine and those whose services have secured them a place in heaven – Hercules, Liber, Aesculapius, Castor, Pollux, Quirinus – and also those qualities on whose account human beings are allowed to ascend to heaven – Good Sense, Moral Excellence, Devotion, Good Faith. In their honour there shall be shrines, but none in honour of vices.

They shall observe the established rites.

On holidays they shall abstain from lawsuits, and they shall hold these holidays in the company of their slaves when their tasks have been finished; and so that it may occur thus let it be arranged at recurrent intervals throughout the year. The priests shall offer in public certain crops and certain fruits – this according to fixed rites and on fixed days. (20) Likewise they shall keep for other days an abundance of milk and young; and to ensure that this be not transgressed the priests shall lay down the procedure and the annual sequence for that sacrifice and they shall decide which victims are appropriate and welcome to each divinity.

Different divinities shall have different priests; all together shall have pontiffs; individually they shall have flamines. And in the city the vestal Virgins shall watch over the undying fire on the public hearth.

Those who are unfamiliar with the methods and rituals for conducting these private and public ceremonies shall seek guidance from the public priests. Of these there shall be three kinds: one to preside over ceremonies and sacred rites, and another to interpret the strange utterances of prophets and seers which the Senate and people have accepted. In addition, the interpreters of Jupiter the Best and Greatest, that is, the public augurs, shall divine the future by means of signs and omens and maintain their art. (21) And the priests shall pay attention to vineyards and patches of withies and the safety of the people. They shall give prior warning about omens to those who are engaged in the business of war or state, and those groups shall take heed of them. They shall foresee the anger of the gods and react appropriately. They shall take measures to neutralise flashes of lightning in fixed quarters of the sky, and they shall keep the city and the countryside and their ancestral fields of observation mapped out and free of obstruction. And whatever an augur shall pronounce unjust, unholy, harmful, or ill-omened shall be null and void. And if anyone fails to obey, that shall be a capital offence.

The fetial priests shall act as judges in the name of the people concerning the ratification of treaties, peace, war and truces; and they shall decide about questions of war.

Prodigies and portents shall, if the senate so decrees, be referred to Etruscan soothsayers, and Etruria shall instruct her leading men in that art. They shall sacrifice in expiation to whatever gods they think fit, and they shall also make atonement in response to flashes of lightning and to the striking of certain places.

No nocturnal sacrifices shall be conducted by women except those which shall take place on behalf of the people; and they shall initiate no one into any mysteries, except those of Ceres through the Greek rite, as custom allows.

(22) An act of sacrilege which cannot be expiated shall be deemed to have been imperiously committed; that which can be expiated shall be expiated by the official priests.

In public games, when there is no chariot racing and no athletic competitions, they shall make provision for the people's joy by singing, accompanied by strings and pipes, and they shall associate that pleasure with the honour of the gods.

Of ancestral rites they shall observe the best.

Except for the slaves of the Idean Mother (and in their case only on specially appointed days) no one shall take up collections.

Anyone who steals or makes away with a sacred object or an object lodged in a sacred place shall be deemed a parricide.

The divine punishment of perjury is death, the human punishment disgrace.

That priests shall inflict the ultimate penalty on the person found guilty of incest.

Let not an impious man dare to placate the gods' anger with the gifts.

Let them be scrupulous in fulfilling their vows; there shall be a penalty for breaking a promise.

No one should consecrate a field. Let there be moderation in dedicating gold, silver, and ivory.

Private religious observances shall be continued in perpetuity.

The rights of the spirits of the dead shall be holy. Good men who have died shall be held to be gods. The money spent on them, and the mourning over them, shall be kept small. (tr. Niall Rudd, Penguin, 1998)

But the outcome is problematic. Cicero's use of an administrative hierarchy as a model on which to represent religion gives the multitude of gods and religious options a significance that he himself is finally incapable of resolving. He falls into the trap awaiting every definition of religion along narrow, political, and/or functional lines: in failing to acknowledge the real level of religious pluralism already present in Rome in the first century BCE, in the sense of religious diversity predicated upon levels of religious engagement, in a society in which religion is postulated as having an integrative power, such an approach also misses the possibility of determining the particularities of specific religious practices and conceptions.[44]

At this point it is possible to summarize that, as far as possible, Cicero models his suggested sequence of religious practices in Book 2 on the "constitution" he discusses in Book 3. This may possibly also explain the dominance of stipulations relating to priesthoods, of which Cicero claims to provide a complete list (2.32), whereas he does not make this claim in his discussion of gods and rituals. The authors of the *lex Ursonensis* a decade later followed a similar procedure, dealing with "religion" in places that, while in themselves appropriate, were uncoordinated.[45] The latter statute also reflects the practice adopted by Varro in modelling the structure of the *Divine Antiquities* on that of the *Human Antiquities*, discussing people, places, periods, and objects, and departing from that rule only in the final books on the gods.[46]

I cannot here enter into a closer analysis of all details of the *constitutio religionum* as presented by the figure of Marcus. It is sufficient to say that his arguments rely on the venerable antiquity of traditions, their historical success (for example in divinatory matters),[47] and, often introduced in the form of a rhetorical question, the supposedly self-evident standards of the Roman elite of the day. He not infrequently cites Plato,[48] who may also have provided the model for the function of religion in society that Marcus here seeks to reconcile with Roman realities. While Cicero was able to rely on the earlier Roman treatises *De magistratibus* and *De potestatibus* as sources for the substantial earlier and lost later part of his third book, we know of no comparable *De religione* for the second book.[49] In traditional Roman law as in Cicero, the formulation of norms is not deductive, but intuitive and casuistic.[50]

---

[44] For a critique of functional approaches to religion (based on E. Durkheim or system theory), see Knoblauch 1999, 116–17.

[45] See Rüpke 2006c.

[46] See Aug. *Civ.* 6.3; more details in Rüpke 2007b, 59–61.

[47] See Cic. *Leg.* 2.32–3.

[48] E.g. for the principles underlying dedications in 2.45.

[49] For possible Greek sources see Dyck 2004, 12–15, although he does not go into Latin texts on Roman practices here; see also 50–2. In 3.49 Cicero points to M. Iunius (Gracchanus) for the subsequent section *de potestatum iure* (3.48). Rawson 1973, 345–6 mentions Ap. Claudius on augural matters, and Laelius' speech on priesthoods from 146 BCE.

[50] See Sauer 2007, 252–3 (after Max Kaser) for this characterization of Cicero, and on Roman law in general.

The problem of deviance and sanctions against it is already addressed in the first sentence (2.19): the gods are to be approached *caste*, in a state of purity. Piety is important, wealth should be kept at a distance. Infringements of the norm are punished by the injured deity himself.[51] This is an ancient principle.[52]

The next stipulation is of especial interest to us, and I duly cite it once more:

> Separatim nemo habessit deos neve novos neve advenas nisi publice adscitos; privatim colunto quos rite a patribus <acceperint>.[53]

Separatim signifies "individual" as opposed to *publice*. It is distinct from *privatim*, which specifically signifies a traditional family cult led by a *pater*. Commentaries on the passage, not only Cicero's own but also those by modern authors, are astoundingly succinct. Cicero argues that "confusion of *religiones*" must be avoided (2.25), a rather non-specific, although incisive, turn of phrase: "anarchy" is simply the opposite of order.[54] In order to avoid the rise of ignorance in the priesthood – and this is Cicero's second argument – priests must have a comprehensive knowledge of religion; nowhere else is this position attested, not even as an ideal. Cicero himself nevertheless asserts no less at the beginning of his list of priests (2.20) and in the associated commentary (2.30): here, everything concerning the private and the public cult is taught by the priests. They are the medium through which knowledge is transferred. They are even indispensable to every form of the private cult. The conclusion is clear: lack of knowledge is the most important cause of deviant religious behaviour. It is the function of the institutional framework to ensure that traditional ritual is perpetuated in its optimum form. This is emphasized in 2.22: *Ex patriis ritibus optuma colunto* ("Of the ancestral rites the best shall be preserved").

Social control of the cult is implicit in the next sentence, calling for the establishment of identifiable cult sites in the countryside and the home as well as the city (2.19). This tradition is confirmed by the banning of the Bacchanalia (which I understand here as a rule that applied to places rather than festivals) in 186 BCE, and the later Imperial charge of atheism against the Christians, who lacked identifiable, permanent sites for their

---

[51] Giving a new monotheistic turn to the passage, Lactantius assiduously notes the use of the masculine singular *deus* (*Div. inst.* 5.20.3).

[52] Cic. *Leg.* 2.25.

[53] Cic. *Leg.* 2.19; Madvig even integrates *cultus acceperint*.

[54] The contradistinction between *ius religionum* and *confusio* is sharply defined in Cic. *Dom.* 127.

cult. Cicero, however, proposes a different purpose: the visible presence of the gods makes the people more pious.[55]

The next point in sequence is Cicero's interest in the continuity of the family cult, clearly referring to a legal problem that had already been commented on in the previous century, and to the later speech on the observance of feast days (*feriae*, 2.19). Meanwhile, he forbids the veneration of vices (as opposed to the cult of virtues), criticizing even traditional cults of this kind in his commentary (2.28).

After his detailed description of priesthoods, Cicero returns to a list of prohibitions. Women are not to perform nocturnal sacrifices, except in the context of publicly ordained rituals; and no one is to be initiated except into the cult of Greek Ceres, thus Eleusinian Demeter (2.21). This gives rise in the commentary to intensive debate on the universal validity of the law (2.35–7), but this need interest us no further. I will concentrate instead on the final section. Here, Cicero links prohibitions with explicit sanctions. In terms of vocabulary, the text suggests an enumeration of religious crimes, as every sentence begins with different categories of religious outrage: *Sacrum ... qui clepsit, periurii, incestum, impius*; *caute* alone returns to positive mode, only to be followed by *poena* (2.22). And yet the text is far from being so systematic. To conceal this, Cicero avoids all discussion in his commentary (2.41). In any event, he clearly associates such extraordinary crimes as offending the modesty of a Vestal Virgin with a general misdemeanour such as the bribing of the gods by wicked people. The formulaic "he shall not dare" and the absence of a sanction in this instance reveal the status of the rule. *Sacrilegium*, the theft or plunder of the property of the gods, and perjury are much clearer categories. The first incurs the death penalty, the second dishonour. Cicero returns full circle to where he began.

He advises – again, we understand, to counter evident deviance – that the supervision of private cults be permanent (literally eternal), and that (again, private) graves be respected (2.22).

I shall attempt to summarize. Like Varro (who, I should like to remind the reader, wrote only a few years later), Cicero is here transforming religion into knowledge. Law is the conceptual form he uses for this undertaking: an "epistemic revolution"[56] that began in the

---

[55] The relevant passage has been subject to many textual emendations. The text that we have could mean that a child (*infans*) is highly religious when it sees gods everywhere; alternatively, it could mean that people are at their most pious at religious sites (*in fanis*).

[56] Ando 2006, 135.

second century BCE. This knowledge is perpetuated and further refined by a number of public priesthoods not always to be identified with senators. We can be sure that this was intended as a form of social control over private affairs. The discourse of public and private is used and at the same time rendered inoperative. Cicero attempts to conceal the pragmatic intention of his religious "constitution" by having it precede the political constitution, which, as I have shown above, serves as a model. Here, Varro chooses the path of greater intellectual clarity and honesty.

From his pragmatic standpoint, Cicero is not engaging in thought-games about the religion of a new-found Roman polity. He is arguing at a period of enormous religious change, conceptualized as deviance. Citizens themselves are introducing new cults and relinquishing older ones. Or, to use a metaphor: his contemporaries are tweeting in a code that the police cannot yet decipher. Religion can be used for private purposes, and is even useful to wrongdoers. In practice, and in view of all these dangers, association of religious activity with established cult sites is vital. But, here too, as we shall see, Cicero is ambivalent.

Summary

The texts discussed so far do not embrace all normative declarations, nor do they analyse the known occurrences of deviant behaviour I have referred to above. It is, therefore, important to contextualize our findings so far. The state of intellectual development of the late Roman Republic is the most important context I have stressed, but a further context is suggested by one observation at least. Remarkably, the normative texts address the outer limits of Roman religion: and there are other religions out there, according to Varro. Cicero's purpose, on occasion at least, is universalization. These texts are accompaniments to the rise of a world empire. Many religious practices of the period – *evocatio* and the rituals of the ambassador-like fetials, triumphs, and the validity of auspices – are concerned with problems arising from that process. We must bear this factor in mind as we analyse changes in the subsequent period.

Within these developments and changes, professional bearers of traditions seem to gain in importance. It is in respect of the priesthoods, perhaps construed on the model of magistrates, that Cicero claims exhaustiveness in his treatment of religion. They are the guarantors of the correct fulfilment of religious duties. However, their central position as conceptualized by Cicero opens up new opportunities of avoiding deviance at the same time as inviting it.

CHAPTER 3

The role of ethos and knowledge in controlling religious deviance

Republican concepts of priesthood

In the vision of religious norms and the concept of religious knowledge developed by Cicero and Varro and analysed in the preceding chapter public priests (*sacerdotes*) were given an important role. We now have to inquire into the status of these bearers of ritual roles and the basis for the function allotted to them by the 50s and 40s of the first century BCE. I will start with a short review of Republican authors before I turn to the first book of Valerius Maximus, which offers the unique possibility of seeing into the thinking of an educated public well below the ranks of the priests and of those aspiring to public priesthoods in the early Principate.

Relevant Latin sources are scarce before the first century BCE. The *sacerdos* of Plautus' *Rudens* should not be violated (646, 655, 671), but is not further characterized. In the earliest epigraphic attestation, the honour of "bearing the flamen's apex", his special headdress, is stressed, pointing nicely to the precise subject of conflict in the late third-century cases reviewed before.[1] This is surprisingly close to the speeches composed by Livy for the arguments about the admission of plebeians to the consulate and the *Xviri sacris faciundis* in 367 BCE (6.41.9). It is the loss of this headdress that causes or metaphorically signifies the loss of the priesthood in incidences from the end of the third century BCE in Augustan authors.[2]

In Varro's etymological treatment of priests in his *On the Latin Language*, priests in general are defined by their ritual activities (5.83–6):

> Sacerdotes uniuersi a sacris dicti. pontufices, ut [a] Scaevola Quintus pontufex maximus dicebat, a posse et facere, ut po[n]tifices. ego a ponte arbitror: nam ab his sublicius est factus primum ut restitutus saepe, cum

---

[1] *CIL* 6.1288: *Qui apice insigne Dial<is fl>aminis gesistei.* See also *Année Epigraphique* 1987,163 with *FS* 2129.

[2] E.g. Hor. *Carm.* 1.34.14 f.; see Rüpke 2010b.

ideo sacra et uls et cis Tiberim non mediocri ritu fiant. (84) curiones dicti a curiis, qui fiunt ut in his sacra faciant. flamines, quod in Latio capite uelato erant semper ac caput cinctum habebant filo, filamines dicti. horum singuli cognomina habent ab eo deo cui sacra faciunt; sed partim sunt aperta, partim obscura: aperta ut Martialis, Volcanalis; obscura Dialis et Furinalis, cum Dialis ab Iove sit (Diovis enim), Furinalis a Furrina, cuius etiam in fastis feriae Furinales sunt. sic flamen Falacer a divo patre Falacre. (85) Salii ab salitando, quod facere in comitiis in sacris quotannis et solent et debent. Luperci, quod Lupercalibus in lupercali sacra faciunt. fratres arbales dicti qui sacra publica faciunt propterea ut fruges ferant arba: a ferendo et aruis fratres aruales dicti. sunt qui a fratria dixerunt. fratria est graecum uocabulum partis hominum, ut Neapoli etiam nunc. sodales Titii dicti ... quas in auguriis certis obseruare solent. (86) fetiales, quod fidei publicae inter populos praeerant: nam per hos fiebat ut iustum conciperetur bellum et †inde desitum, ut foedere fides pacis constitueretur. ex his mittebantur, ante quam conciperetur, qui res repeterent, et per hos etiam nunc fit foedus, quod fidus Ennius scribit dictum.

(83) The priests collectively were named from the sacred rites. The pontiffs, Quintus Scaevola the Pontifex Maximus said, were named from "to be able" and "to do", as though *potentifices*. For my part I think that the name comes from "bridge"; for by them the Bridge on Piles was made in the first place, and it was likewise repeatedly repaired by them, since in that connexion rites are performed on both sides of the Tiber with no small ceremony. The *curiones* were named from the *curiae*; they are created for conducting sacred rites in the *curiae*.

(84) The flamines, because in Latium they always kept their heads covered and had their hair girt with a woollen "band", were originally called *filamines*. Individually they have distinguishing epithets from that god whose rites they perform; but some are obvious, others obscure: obvious, like Martialis and Volcanalis; obscure are Dialis and Furinalis, since Dialis is from Jove, for he is called also Diovis, and Furinalis from Furrina, who even has a Furinal Festival in the calendar. So also the Flamen Falacer from the divine father Falacer.

(85) The *salii* were named from *salitare*, "to dance", because they had the custom and the duty of dancing yearly in the assembly-places, in their ceremonies. The Luperci were so named because they make offerings in the Lupercal at the festival of the Lupercalia. "Arval brothers" was the name given to those who perform public rites to the end that the ploughlands may bear fruits: from *ferre* (to bear) and *arua* (ploughlands) they are called *fratres arvales*. But some have said that they were named from *fratria* (brotherhood): *fratria* is the Greek name of a part of the people, as at Naples even now. The "Titian comrades" are so named ... from the twittering birds which they are accustomed to watch in some of their augural observations.

(86) The herald-priests, because they were in charge of the state's word of honour in matters between peoples; for by them it was brought about that a war that was declared should be a just war, and by them the war was stopped, that by a treaty the "honesty" of the peace might be established. Some of them were sent before war should be declared, to demand restitution of the stolen property, and by them even now is made the "treaty" which Ennius writes was pronounced *fidus*. (tr. Roland G. Kent, Loeb, 1938, with corrections)

Again, it is the headdress that offers a possibility of an etymology for the *flamines*; the sequence and the wording do not point to any further categorization of the priests. In the *Antiquitates rerum diuinarum* it is the first triad (Books 2–4) that deals with the priesthoods as "humans", following the structure men – places – times – things (now: *sacra*) of the preceding *Antiquitates rerum humanarum* (fr. 4 Cardauns). One of the few fragments of these books, and one explicitly related to Book 2, addresses the *flamen Dialis* as a member of the pontifical college.[3]

In the *Antiquitates*, however, we can detect a trait that is very prominent in another writer, Varro's contemporary. The priests are responsible for the public cult, but they do not have only to administer it; they are also responsible for knowledge about it (fr. 9 Cardauns). Both, knowledge and ritual, form the third type of theology, the *theologia ciuilis*:[4]

> Tertium genus est ... quod in urbibus ciues, maxime sacerdotes, nosse atque administrare debent. In quo est, quos deos publice † sacra ac sacrificia colere et facere quemque par sit.

> The third type is ... what in the cities the citizens, and above all the priests, have to know and administrate. This consists of knowing which gods it is reasonable to care for by rituals and sacrifices from public money, and by whom (?). (tr. J. Rüpke)

In the beginning of the same first book, Varro compares himself to a famous priest, Caecilius Metellus, who had rescued the sacred objects from the burning sanctuary of Vesta. The component of knowledge and its preservation is even more valuable than mere ritual continuity.[5]

The contemporary I have referred to is Cicero. In his attempt at a systematic ruling on religion in the second book of his *On the Laws*,

---

[3] Varro, *Ant. rer. div.* fr. 51 Cardauns: *Is solum album habet galerum, vel quod maximus, vel quod Iovi immolata hostia alba id fieri oporteat.*
[4] Rüpke 2005b.
[5] Varro *Ant. rer. div.* fr. 2, see Rüpke 2012a, 174 f.

probably written a few years earlier than Varro's *Antiquities*, knowledge is paramount, and most peculiar to the *sacerdotes publici*. It is here that his norms and his commentary aim at completeness; it is here that he tries to define the intersection of the public cult and the vast area of private cult, and to establish control of the latter. Only if the *sacerdotes publici* know all about currently maintained private cults can they be a helpful resource for private people in religious matters.[6] As I have argued above, Cicero was probably inspired by the systematic treatment developed in Book 3 in respect of magistrates.[7] The figure of Attus Navius in *On Divination* is a prototype of that same systematic, projected into earliest times (1.32).

Religion and priests in Valerius Maximus

Writing under the emperor Tiberius, Valerius Maximus undertook the huge task of collecting "memorable deeds and sayings" by sifting through a large amount of late Republican and Augustan literature.[8] His aim being moral improvement,[9] his hope was that the examples of virtuous people from earlier history would provide a powerful resource for contemporary society. The careful thematic arrangement of books and chapters, in examples from Rome and elsewhere, reflects the spread of historical argumentation beyond aristocrats who had full control over what their *maiores* had done or would not have done.[10]

The exemplary behaviour cited is certainly that of those aristocrats; but there is a shift in authority. In the very first sentence Valerius stresses his concern that those interested in first-hand documents (*documenta sumere uolentibus*) should be spared the trouble of undertaking time-consuming studies (1, pr.). Foreign instances are assigned to second place in every class of examples, but, from the beginning of the work per se, *urbis Romae exterarumque gentium facta simul ac dicta memoratu digna* are both documented in a series of *domesticae peregrinaeque historiae*, a treasury of "history both made at home and imported", as the phrase shortly following might be rendered (1, pr.). Only a universal history *(omnis aeui gesta)* could suffice for the empire of the early Principate. It is just such a historical work that Valerius dedicates to him with whom *hominum deorumque*

---

[6] See Chapter 2, section "Cicero".
[7] See Chapter 2, section "Cicero".
[8] Some of the following arguments are derived from Rüpke 2015b.
[9] Skidmore 1996; Lucarelli 2007.
[10] Krasser 2005.

consensus maris ac terrae regimen, the "consensus of men and gods and the ruling of sea and land", i.e. to Caesar (1, pr.), i.e. to Tiberius.

Religion plays an important role in Valerius' enterprise: "the condition of the cult of the gods", as the author's introductory, titular sentence might be reordered,[11] is the topic of the first volume. Maintaining the geographical orientation, the opening passage gives a great deal of attention to location. Religion, for Valerius, is not confined to the city of Rome or *ager Romanus*. It is universal (1.1.1):

> Maiores statas sollemnesque caerimonias pontificum scientia, bene gerendarum rerum auctoritates augurum obseruatione, Apollinis praedictiones uatum libris, portentorum depulsi<one>s Etrusca disciplina explicari uoluerunt. prisco etiam instituto rebus diuinis opera datur, cum aliquid conmendandum est, precatione, cum exposcendum, uoto, cum soluendum, gratulatione, cum inquirendum uel extis uel sortibus, inpetrito, cum sollemni ritu peragendum, sacrificio, quo etiam ostentorum ac fulgurum denuntiationes procurantur.
>
> Tantum autem studium antiquis non solum seruandae sed etiam amplificandae religionis fuit, ut florentissima tum et opulentissima ciuitate decem principum filii senatus consulto singulis Etruriae populis percipiendae sacrorum disciplinae gratia traderentur, Cererique, quam more Graeco uenerari instituerant, sacerdotem a Velia, cum id oppidum nondum ciuitatem accepisset, nomine Calliphanam peterent [uel, ut alii dicunt, Calliphoenam], ne deae uetustis ritibus perita deesset antistes.
>
> Cuius cum in urbe pulcherrimum templum haberent, Gracchano tumultu moniti Sibyllinis libris ut uetustissimam Cererem placarent, Hennam, quoniam sacra eius inde orta credebant, X uiros ad eam propitiandam miserunt. item Matri deum saepe numero imperatores nostri conpotes uictoriarum suscepta uota Pessinuntem profecti soluerunt.

Our ancestors wanted fixed and customary ceremonies to be regulated by the knowledge of the pontiffs, authorizations for the successful conduct of affairs by the observations of the augurs, the prophecies of Apollo by the books of the seers, and the averting of omens by the Etruscan discipline. Also by ancient practice attention is paid to the divine: through prayer when anything requires entrusting to the gods; through a vow when a favour is to be requested; through a ceremony of thanksgiving when a vow is to be paid; through receipt of a favourable omen when it is necessary to consult either entrails or oracles; through sacrifice (by which also the warnings of prodigies and lightning-strikes are averted) when a customary rite is to be performed.

---

[11] Val. Max. 1, pr., end: *Et quoniam initium a cultu deorum petere in animo est, de condicitone eius summatim disseram.*

Among the ancients the desire for not only preserving but also increasing worship was so great that, when the state was very flourishing and very wealthy, by a decree of the Senate the sons of ten leading citizens were entrusted to the individual peoples of Etruria in order to learn the lore of the sacred rites; and for Ceres (whom they had begun to worship in the Greek fashion), they asked for a priestess named Calliphana [or, as others say, Calliphoena] from Velia, when that town had not yet acquired Roman citizenship, in order that the ancient rites of the goddess should not lack a skilled priestess. Although they had a very beautiful temple to her in the city, at the time of the Gracchan troubles warned by the Sibylline Books to placate the most ancient Ceres, they sent the Board of Ten to Enna to win her over, since they believed that her rites came from there. Similarly, in honour of the Mother of the gods, when our generals have won victories, they have often gone to Pessinus and paid the vows they had undertaken. (tr. David Wardle, Clarendon, 1998)

The whole passage is heavily relyiant on Ciceronian pretexts.[12] And yet, the arrangement and the systematics of rites is original. The most obvious dimension of this passage is geographical. The religion, the "condition of the cult" Valerius is interested in, is not confined to the city of Rome or *ager Romanus*. Religion too is universal, and Valerius here concurs with other delineations of the history of religion by Roman authors.[13]

Religious knowledge

In respect of authority, I am more interested in another feature of the text, the stress on knowledge. *Pontificum scientia*, "the knowledge of the pontiffs", the keen "empirical attentiveness of the augurs" (*augurum obseruatione*), the "books of the prophets" (*uatum libris*), and, finally, "Etruscan science" (*Etrusca disciplina*), set the tone. Despite a traditionalist orientation visible in many phrases, innovation is built into the system. It was always an ancient habit not only to preserve religion but to enlarge it. Innovation is driven by knowledge. It is the concern of the priests.

If this is the message, it is driven home by the examples that follow. The very next of these teaches that *caerimoniis Martis* is more important than *Martio certamini*: cult duties to Mars at home are more important than martial competition on the battlefield (1.1.2). It is the *pontifex maximus* – a function of Caesar at Valerius' time, we have to remind ourselves – who is in charge of these priorities, even against a fellow priest.

---

[12] Wardle 1998, 75–86, in particular Cic. *Resp.* 18; *Diu.* 1.92; *Balb.* 55.
[13] See my analysis of the fragments of Varro's *Antiquitates rerum divinarum* in Rüpke 2012b.

It is, however, not the person of the priest, but the role of knowledge that is of paramount importance. The next example is designed to reiterate that message, although it is frequently quoted for its factual content only (1.1.3).[14] By reading books about the public cult, Tiberius Gracchus detected a ritual mistake that was made in an act for which he was responsible; in exemplary fashion, he did not confine himself to reading, but wrote to the college of augurs, whose deliberations resulted in a report to the Senate, who in turn ordered the consuls to return from the provinces in order to abdicate. Deviance has to be precisely qualified, and is punished as an error, thus opening up the possibility of ritual redress:

> Laudabile duodecim fascium religiosum obsequium, laudabilior quattuor et XX in consimili re oboedientia: a Tiberio enim Graccho ad collegium augurum litteris ex prouincia missis, quibus significabat se, cum libros ad sacra populi pertinentes legeret, animaduertisse uitio tabernaculum captum comitiis consularibus, quae ipse fecisset, eaque re ab auguribus ad senatum relata iussu eius C. Figulus e Gallia, Scipio Nasica e Corsica Romam redierunt et se consulatu abdicauerunt.

> The submission of the twelve rods to religion was laudable; more laudable was the obedience of the twenty-four in a similar situation. For letters were sent by Tiberius Gracchus from his province to the college of augurs, in which he informed them that, when he was reading the books relating to public ceremonies, he had noticed that for the consular elections, which he himself had held, the tent had been set up incorrectly. The matter was reported to the Senate by the augurs and, on its order, C. Figulus returned to Rome from Gaul and Scipio Nasica from Corsica, and they abdicated the consulship. (tr. Wardle)

Another famous incident is related subsequently.[15] The effort to parallel and further the expansion of the empire by religious activities has to be checked by attention given to religious detail, a concern laudable in itself. This is achieved by the college of pontiffs, even against somebody who is consul for the fifth time, successful in the field, and pious. Neither the huge prestige of the man nor the additional costs incurred prevented the college from delivering its "admonition".[16] Marcellus, victor at Clastidium and Syracuse, built two *cellae* in his temple to Honor and Virtue (1.1.8):

---

[14] The passage includes details lacking in the Ciceronian accounts and might stem from Livy (Wardle 1998, 89).
[15] Val. Max. 1.1.8.
[16] See Flower 2003, 46 for the role within the image of Marcellus (see also Flower 2000).

Non mirum igitur, si pro eo imperio augendo custodiendoque pertinax deorum indulgentia semper excubuit, quo tam scrupulosa cura paruula quoque momenta religionis examinari uidentur, quia numquam remotos ab exactissimo cultu caerimoniarum oculos habuisse nostra ciuitas existimanda est. in qua cum <M.> Marcellus quintum consulatum gerens templum Honori et Virtuti Clastidio prius, deinde Syracusis potitus nuncupatis debitum uotis consecrare uellet, a collegio pontificum inpeditus est, negante unam cellam duobus diis recte dicari: futurum enim, si quid prodigii in ea accidisset, ne dinosceretur utri rem diuinam fieri oporteret, nec duobus nisi certis diis una sacrificari solere. ea pontificum admonitione effectum est ut Marcellus separatis aedibus Honoris ac Virtutis simulacra statueret, neque aut collegio pontificum auctoritas amplissimi uiri aut Marcello adiectio inpensae inpedimento fuit quo minus religionibus suus tenor suaque obseruatio redderetur.

So it is not surprising if the persevering goodwill of the gods has been eternally vigilant on behalf of the increase and preservation of that empire where even minutely small questions of religion are seen to be examined with so scrupulous a concern, because our state must never be thought to have averted its eyes from the most exact performance of rites. In this state when <M.> Marcellus, during his fifth consulship, having captured first Clastidium and then Syracuse, wanted to consecrate a temple to Honour and Courage in fulfilment of vows he had solemnly taken, he was prevented by the college of pontiffs which said that one chamber could not rightly be dedicated to two gods: for if some prodigy were to happen in it, they would not be able to determine to which sacrifice should be made; nor was it customary to make one sacrifice to two gods, except for defined gods. The result of that instruction by the pontiffs was that Marcellus set up cult-images of Honour and Courage in separate temples. Neither for the college of pontiffs did the influence of a very distinguished man nor for Marcellus did the increase in expense prevent the religious institutions being guaranteed their own due continuity and respect. (tr. Wardle)

Such knowledge is effective only when controlled. The famous story of the sarcophagus of Numa, which was found in the early second century, is related by Valerius with respect to the peculiar circumstance that the seven Latin books on pontifical law were carefully preserved, but the seven Greek books on philosophy burned, as they might turn people away from their cult observances (1.1.12 f.):[17]

Magna conseruandae religionis etiam P. Cornelio Baebio Tamphilo consulibus apud maiores nostros acta cura est. si quidem in agro L. Petili scribae

---

[17] Cf. Rosenberger 2003.

sub Ianiculo cultoribus terram altius uersantibus, duabus arcis lapideis repertis, quarum in altera scriptura indicabat corpus Numae Pompili fuisse, in altera libri reconditi erant Latini septem de iure pontificum totidemque Graeci de disciplina sapientiae, Latinos magna diligentia adseruandos curauerunt, Graecos, quia aliqua ex parte ad soluendam religionem pertinere existimabantur, Q. Petilius praetor urbanus ex auctoritate senatus per uictimarios facto igni in conspectu populi cremauit: noluerunt enim prisci uiri quidquam in hac adseruari ciuitate, quo animi hominum a deorum cultu auocarentur.

In the consulship of Publius Cornelius and Baebius Tamphilus our ancestors showed great scruples in their respect for religion. When farm-hands were digging rather deeply in a field under the Janiculum belonging to a scribe called Lucius Petillius, they found two stone chests. An inscription on one revealed that it contained the body of Numa Pompilius. In the other were found seven Latin books about the law of the pontiffs, and as many Greek books about the discipline of philosophy. They ordered that the Latin books should be preserved with the greatest care, but they felt that the Greek ones might in some way tend to undermine religion. Following Senate instructions, the city praetor, Quintus Petillius, ordered the sacrificial attendants to make a fire and burn the books in public. The men of those days did not want to retain anything in this state that might take people's minds away from the worship of the gods. (tr. Walker)

Options that do not lead to knowledge that is controllable are removed. Again, deviancy is sharply sanctioned. The example immediately following gives even more profile to the management of knowledge: not only does it require preservation, but undue proliferation too has to be curbed (1.1.13):

Tarquinius autem rex M. Atilium duumuirum, quod librum secreta ri<tu>um ciuilium sacrorum continentem, custodiae suae conmissum corruptus Petronio Sabino describendum dedisset, culleo insutum in mare abici iussit, idque supplicii genus multo post parricidis lege inrogatum est, iustissime quidem, quia pari uindicta parentum ac deorum uiolatio expianda est.

King Tarquin ordered M. Atilius, a member of the Board of Two, to be sown into a sack and thrown into the sea because, bribed by Petronius, a Sabine, he had handed over to be copied a book entrusted to his keeping which contained secrets of the civic rites. Much later this kind of punishment was imposed by law on parricides with the utmost appropriateness, because profanation of parents and the gods should be expiated with equal punishments. (tr. Wardle)

This description of the contents of the books clearly deviates from earlier narratives on the function and fate of the Sibylline books.[18] Valerius even avoids the term *libri Sibyllini* in order to create his own version of these early books.

Valerius presents a selection, and construes his image of religion by his very choices. His selection forms the foundation of many accounts of Roman Republican religion. It provides an account of religious ruling taking precedence over anything else, an account of public priests being at the very centre of religion by virtue of their total control of knowledge, and it is an account lacking chronological references: there is change, but it is quantitative, not qualitative change, and is bound up with territorial expansion. Modern historiography of religion has rather neglected the existence of the first kind of change, and rather accepted the suppression of the second.[19] With regard to our topic, and to the dimension of change we are concerned with in this volume, we are not entitled to repeat this oversight.

Valerius' knowledgeable priests are the priests of Cicero's time, but they are not the priests of the period before the second, perhaps late second century BCE.[20] Ritual punctiliousness, surely a trait much older than Cicero and one still very important to Valerius Maximus, has been radicalized by the introduction of the concept of knowledge.

A contemporary voice in historical garb

From the point of view of observers in the very late Republican and early Imperial period, the complexities of the divine were a matter of knowledge. And knowledge was the basis upon which the religious resources offered by the divine in the shape of numerous propitious deities were successfully tapped, and religious deviance was avoided. The gods were present as agents about whom one could know something. They continued to be present in the form of narratives, but they could be multiplied, pinned down, given better shape, by virtue of being "known" about.[21] In contrast to mere mythological narrative, the new forms of knowledge

---

[18] Here again Wardle 1998, 108, tries to minimize Valerius' originality.
[19] Cf. the standard handbooks on Roman religion: Wissowa 1912; Bayet 1957; Latte 1960; Scheid 1998; Beard, North, and Price 1998; Rüpke 2007b.
[20] See Rüpke 2011a and 2012a on processes of rationalization in late Republican religion; cf. Beard, North, and Price 1998, 108–13.
[21] Cf. Varro, *Ant. rer. div.* fr. 3: *pro ingenti beneficio ... iactat praestare se ciuibus suis, quia non solum commemorate deos, quos coli oportet a Romanis, uerum etiam dicit, quid ad quemque pertineat.*

could assimilate different types of discourse, and integrate shared knowledge about gods. Varro's three types of theology offered one account of a way of organizing such knowledge,[22] Cicero in the *De legibus* another.[23] Rather than a lived tradition of the accumulation of knowledge by priests, it must have been such accounts that had shaped Valerius' imagination.

Knowledge about religion was not only an academic enterprise. It was a concern for divinatory knowledge that led Augustus to burn two thousand oracular books.[24] Astrological knowledge was intensively tapped by the emperor Tiberius himself, in his employment of specialists like Scribonius and Tib. Claudius Thrasyllus.[25] But divinatory knowledge was potentially dangerous.[26] The possession of such knowledge was accordingly defined as deviant or even downright criminal. In 17 CE, *mathematici* were driven out of town together with Jews;[27] some had been executed the previous year in the context of a supposed conspiracy.[28] According to Suetonius, Tiberius demanded that any *haruspex* be consulted in public, and in the presence of witnesses.[29]

Valerius may have reflected this ambivalent status in the composition of his first book. Preserved only in later excerpts in Iulius Paris and Ianuarius Nepotianus (the latter in highly critical mood) is the following, second section, presenting examples of famous Romans who had claimed intimate communication with gods. This section offers a rare account of an exploration of the borderline between narratives of particularly religious and religiously deviant behaviour.

It is impossible to reconstruct the wording of Valerius, but the heading *De simulate religione*, "On pretended worship" (Wardle), is certainly not authentic. The short list of Roman examples is impressive: Valerius deals with Numa, Scipio Africanus, Sulla, Marius, and Q. Sertorius.[30] But Numa's claim to have met the nymph Egeria is as dubious as the white hind that accompanied Sertorius in Spain. Usually, Valerius is very reluctant to present examples from a period as early as Numa, and even more

---

[22] Rüpke 2005a.
[23] Rüpke 2012a, 186–204.
[24] Suet. *Aug.* 31.1.
[25] Suet. *Tib.* 14.2 and 4. See the general judgement in 69: *Circa deos ac religiones neglegentior, quippe addictus mathematicae …*
[26] See pp. 83–85 and Fögen 1993 for the radicalization of the problem from the third century CE onwards.
[27] Suet. *Tib.* 36.
[28] Tac. *Ann.* 2.32.
[29] Suet. *Tib.* 63.
[30] Val. Max. 1.2.1–4.

reluctant to present fantastic elements of such narratives.[31] The literary framing is even more telling. The following section – again bearing a late heading *De superstitionibus* – gives examples of prohibitions of contacts with foreign deities, and even includes a second-century-BCE instance of the expulsion of *Chaldaei*.[32] Only after this section does a new sequence start, dealing with auspices, omens, prodigies, dreams, and miracles, all positively judged and presented as divine voices that should be followed, and are neglected at the peril of negative consequences.[33]

With Valerius Maximus, the discourse on explicitly religious (and not just philosophical and political) deviance reached a new, or at least more explicit, stage. It is now not only religious practices that offer room for legitimate or illegitimate variance;[34] religious knowledge has also reached a critical stage. As already suggested by Cicero, such knowledge should be controlled by priests, but they are also to apply it reflectively to themselves. We are far from any concept of "belief"; but lack of knowledge or deviant knowledge is important, and has consequences. Behaviour is to be judged in the light of the knowledge possessed by religious actors, as we will see in the next chapter.

---

[31] Skidmore 1996, 94–6.
[32] Val. Max. 1.3, in particular 1.3.2.
[33] Val. Max. 1.4–8.
[34] Given the examples, Wardle's (1998, 137 f.) suggestion that Valerius Maximus applied the category of fraud here is too narrow.

CHAPTER 4

De superstitione: *religious experiences best not had in temples*

A false conception of the gods

By focusing on prominent individuals, the moralist and historian Valerius Maximus had been dealing with religious deviance only as an aspect of strategic action in a political or military context. However, the concept of *superstitio* necessitated further reflection. Ancient philosophy and polemic on religious deviance produced entire treatises devoted to this theme. In the Latin tradition, Seneca's text *De superstitione* from the mid-first century CE survives only in fragments. Plutarch of Chaeronea's *Peri deisidaimonia*, probably written only a short time later, in about 70 CE,[1] comes down to us in its entirety. Both texts have been subjected to intensive analysis by philosophers and religious historians,[2] as I have described in the first chapter of this book.

Plutarch's text is known for its juxtaposition of *deisidaimonia* on the one hand and atheism on the other as the two main forms taken by false attitudes to the gods (Ch. 1 = 164E). This antithesis gives the entire text its structure, and leads to a comparison that – astonishingly – favours atheism, as atheism would never lead to superstition, whereas superstition often develops into atheism (Chs 10a–12 = 169E–171B). This has even led to the hypothesis that Plutarch had in mind a diatribe from the third century BCE by the atheist Cynic Bion of Borysthenes.[3] The dominant trait of the superstitious person is fear of the gods, which clearly shows a false conception of them, a misbegotten theology[4] capable, in its lack of discrimination, even of embracing demons. Dale B. Martin, in his attempt

---

[1] Görgemanns 2003, 307 argues strongly that the text is from Plutarch's youth, as does Erbse 1952, 297–304. This remains hypothetical, and should not stand in the way of appreciating the levels of continuity in Plutarch's thinking (Klauck 1994, 65).

[2] E.g. Moellering 1963; Lausberg 1970; Brenk 1977; Lausberg 1989; Baldassarri 1996; Martin 2004; Bowden 2008.

[3] Erbse 1952, 299, after Abernetty 1911.

[4] Erbse 1952, 304–13; Martin 2004, 96.

to pursue the concept of superstition in Greek texts, has rightly recognized that it was only in later texts that Plutarch introduced the concept of *daimones* who might be negatively inclined towards humans; this had consequences, undermining as it did the general line of Plutarch's philosophical argument.[5]

In his early text, Plutarch concentrates on the ambivalence that results when piety is marred by unjustified fear. His choice of examples and his observations allow us insight into the practical concerns of the religion of his time. His analysis begins in the private sphere, in sleep and in the home (3c–d = 165E–166A), but then passes rapidly on to temples. Instead of places of relief in crises, sanctuaries become places of punishment (4a = 166F). This logic of hate and fear, and the search for closeness to the gods (11 = 170E), pervades the entire treatise: *proskynesis* in face of images, instead of a realistic conception of transcendent deities; an attitude that combines criticism of the gods with resort to them (6b = 167) is typical. Staying at home involves a milder manifestation of the *deisidaimonia* (7d = 168D) that can be seen at its most severe in the temples of the gods (9b = 169E).

ἐστεφανωμένος ὠχριᾷ, θύει καὶ φοβεῖται, εὔχεται φωνῇ παλλομένῃ καὶ χερσὶν ἐπιθυμιᾷ τρεμούσαις, καὶ ὅλως ἀποδείκνυσι τὸν Πυθαγόρου λόγον φλύαρον εἰπόντος ὅτι βέλτιστοι γιγνόμεθα πρὸς τοὺς θεοὺς βαδίζοντες· τότε γὰρ ἀθλιώτατα καὶ κάκιστα πράττουσιν οἱ δεισιδαίμονες, ὥσπερ ἄρκτων φωλεοῖς ἢ χειαῖς δρακόντων ἢ μυχοῖς κητῶν τοῖς τῶν θεῶν μεγάροις ἢ ἀνακτόροις προσιόντες.

When the garland is on his head he turns pale, he offers sacrifice and feels afraid, he prays with quavering voice, with trembling hands he sprinkles incense, and, in a word, proves how foolish are the words of Pythagoras, who said that we reach our best when we draw near to the gods. For that is the time when the superstitious fare most miserably and wretchedly, for they approach the halls or temples of the gods as they would approach bears' dens or snakes' holes or the haunts of monsters of the deep. (tr. Frank Cole Babbitt, Loeb, 1928)

The image of Carthaginians sacrificing their own children is the culmination (13 = 171C–E) of the closing analysis of *deisidaimonia* as emotional confusion (14), which is more likely to lead to atheism than to – the final word – *eusebeia* (14 = 171F).

---

[5] Martin 2004, 98–108. Cf. Van Nuffelen 2011, ch. 2.

Οὐκ ἄμεινον οὖν ἦν Γαλάταις ἐκείνοις καὶ Σκύθαις τὸ παράπαν μήτ᾽ ἔννοιαν ἔχειν θεῶν μήτε φαντασίαν μήθ᾽ ἱστορίαν ἢ θεοὺς εἶναι νομίζειν χαίροντας ἀνθρώπων σφαττομένων αἵματι καὶ τελεωτάτην θυσίαν καὶ ἱερουργίαν ταύτην νομίζοντας; τί δέ; Καρχηδονίοις οὐκ ἐλυσιτέλει Κριτίαν λαβοῦσιν ἢ Διαγόραν νομοθέτην ἀπ᾽ ἀρχῆς μήτε τινὰ δαιμόνων μήτε θεῶν νομίζειν ἢ τοιαῦτα θύειν οἷα τῷ Κρόνῳ ἔθυον; οὐχ ὥσπερ Ἐμπεδοκλῆς φησι τῶν τὰ ζῷα θυόντων καθαπτόμενος μορφὴν δ᾽ ἀλλάξαντα πατὴρ φίλον υἱὸν ἀείρασσφάζει ἐπευχόμενος μέγα νήπιος, ἀλλ᾽ εἰδότες καὶ γιγνώσκοντες αὐτοὶ τὰ αὑτῶν τέκνα καθιέρευον, οἱ δ᾽ ἄτεκνοι παρὰ τῶν πενήτων ὠνούμενοι παιδία κατέσφαζον καθάπερ ἄρνας ἢ νεοσσούς, παρειστήκει δ᾽ ἡ μήτηρ ἄτεγκτος καὶ ἀστένακτος. εἰ δὲ στενάξειεν ἢ δακρύσειεν, ἔδει τῆς τιμῆς στέρεσθαι, τὸ δὲ παιδίον οὐδὲν ἧττον ἐθύετο· κρότου τε κατεπίμπλατο πάντα πρὸ τοῦ ἀγάλματος ἐπαυλούντων καὶ τυμπανιζόντων ἕνεκα τοῦ μὴ γενέσθαι τὴν βοὴν τῶν θρήνων ἐξάκουστον. εἰ δὲ Τυφῶνές τινες ἢ Γίγαντες ἦρχον ἡμῶν τοὺς θεοὺς ἐκβαλόντες, ποίαις ἂν ἥδοντο θυσίαις ἢ τίνας ἄλλας ἱερουργίας ἀπήτουν; Ἄμηστρις δ᾽ ἡ Ξέρξου γυνὴ δώδεκα κατώρυξεν ἀνθρώπους ζῶντας ὑπὲρ αὑτῆς τῷ Ἅιδῃ, ὃν ὁ Πλάτων φησὶ φιλάνθρ ωπον ὄντα καὶ σοφὸν καὶ πλούσιον, πειθοῖ καὶ λόγῳ κατέχοντα τὰς ψυχάς, Ἅιδην ὠνομάσθαι. Ξενοφάνης δ᾽ ὁ φυσικὸς τοὺς Αἰγυπτίους κοπτομένους ἐν ταῖς ἑορταῖς καὶ θρηνοῦντας ὁρῶν ὑπέμνησεν οἰκείως. "οὗτοι," φησίν, "εἰ μὲν θεοί εἰσι, μὴ θρηνεῖτε αὐτούς· εἰ δ᾽ ἄνθρωποι, μὴ θύετε αὐτοῖς." (14) Ἀλλ᾽ οὐδὲν οὕτω πολυπλανὲς καὶ πολυπαθὲς νόσημα καὶ μεμιγμένον ἐναντίαις δόξαις καὶ μαχομέναις μᾶλλον ὡς τὸ τῆς δεισιδαιμονίας. φευκτέον οὖν αὐτὴν ἀσφαλῶς τε καὶ συμφερό ντως, οὐχ ὥσπερ οἱ ληστῶν ἢ θηρίων ἔφοδον ἢ πῦρ ἀπερισκέπτως καὶ ἀλογίστως περιφεύγοντες ἐμπίπτουσιν εἰς ἀνοδίας βάραθρα καὶ κρημνοὺς ἐχούσας. οὕτω γὰρ ἔνιοι φεύγοντες τὴν δεισιδαιμονίαν ἐμπίπ τουσιν εἰς ἀθεότητα τραχεῖαν καὶ ἀντίτυπον, ὑπερπηδήσαντες ἐν μέσῳ κειμένην τὴν εὐσέβειαν.

Would it not then have been better for those Gauls and Scythians to have had absolutely no conception, no vision, no tradition, regarding the gods, than to believe in the existence of gods who take delight in the blood of human sacrifice and hold this to be the most perfect offering and holy rite? Again, would it not have been far better for the Carthaginians to have taken Critias or Diagoras to draw up their law-code at the very beginning, and so not to believe in any divine power or god, rather than to offer such sacrifices as they used to offer to Cronos? These were not in the manner that Empedocles describes in his attack on those who sacrifice living creatures: Changed in form is the son beloved of his father so pious, / Who on the altar lays him and slays him. What folly! No, but with full knowledge and understanding they themselves offered up their own children, and those who had no children would buy little ones from poor people and cut their throats as if they were so many lambs or young birds; meanwhile the mother

stood by without a tear or moan; but should she utter a single moan or
let fall a single tear, she had to forfeit the money, and her child was sac-
rificed nevertheless; and the whole area before the statue was filled with a
loud noise of flutes and drums that the cries of wailing should not reach the
ears of the people. Yet, if Typhons or Giants were ruling over us after they
had expelled the gods, with what sort of sacrifices would they be pleased,
or what other holy rites would they require? Amestris, the wife of Xerxes,
caused twelve human beings to be buried alive as an offering in her behalf
to propitiate Hades, of whom Plato says that it is because he is humane and
wise and rich, and controls the souls of the dead by persuasion and reason,
that he has come to be called by this name. Xenophanes, the natural philosopher, seeing the Egyptians beating their breasts and wailing at their festivals, gave them a very proper suggestion: "If these beings are gods," said he,
"do not bewail them; and if they are men, do not offer sacrifices to them."
(14) But there is no infirmity comprehending such a multitude of errors and
emotions, and involving opinions so contradictory, or rather antagonistic,
as that of superstition. We must try, therefore, to escape it in some way
which is both safe and expedient, and not be like people who incautiously
and blindly run hither and thither to escape from an attack of robbers or
wild beasts, or from a fire, and rush into trackless places that contain pitfalls
and precipices. For thus it is that some persons, in trying to escape superstition, rush into a rough and hardened atheism, thus overleaping true religion
which lies between. (tr. Frank Cole Babbitt, Loeb, 1928)

Plutarch's selection of instances could nevertheless be seen as fortuitous if
it were not for the example of Seneca's text, written a few decades earlier,[6]
and which Plutarch is unlikely to have known. One of the few extant fragments of Seneca's *De superstitione* concerns comparable practices, as, for
example, the washing and combing of a statue:[7]

In Capitolium perueni, pudebit publicatae dementiae, quod sibi uanus
furor adtribuit officii. Alius nomina deo subicit, alius horas Ioui nun-
tiat: alius lutor est, alius unctor, qui uano motu bracchiorum imitatur
unguentem. Sunt quae Iunoni ac Mineruae capillos disponant (longe a
templo, non tantum a simulacro stantes digitos mouent ornantium modo),
sunt quae speculum teneant; sunt qui ad uadimonia sua deos aduocent,
sunt qui libellos offerant et illos causam suam doceant. Doctus archimi-
mus, senex iam decrepitus, cotidie in Capitolio mimum agebat, quasi dii

---

[6] André 1983, 57 argues for a late date for Seneca's treatise, pointing to the broad basis of the work's
polemic. An absolute dating is not possible (Lausberg 1989, 1898). If the work belonged to the late
fifties or sixties it would be separated by about three decades from a Plutarchian piece (perhaps)
written in the Flavian period.

[7] Sen. *Superst.* fr. 36 Haase = fr. 69 Vottero (Aug. *Civ.* 6.10).

libenter spectarent, quem illi homines desierant. Omne illic artificum genus operatum diis inmortalibus desidet.

Go up to the Capitol! One is ashamed of the lunacy that is displayed there publicly, because sheer madness hides behind the pretence of duty. While one idiot whispers names in the god's ear, another informs Jupiter of the time of day. Here is a bather, there an anointer, miming the act of anointing with empty movements of his arms. Women arrange Juno's and Minerva's hair (they stand far away from the temple, let alone the statue, and move their fingers in imitation of hairdressers); there are women holding mirrors, men calling for the gods' presence at their court hearings, others showing them their witness statements, and acquainting them with their cases. A learned arch-mime, already weak with age, performed his mime daily on the Capitol, as if the gods were eager to see the act that mortals scorned. Artists of every kind wish to have their moment of fame in front of the immortal gods. (tr. J. Rüpke/D. Richardson)

The following fragment, likewise readily cited by Augustine, makes clearer the emotional element of the ritual performances of the various actors:

Hi tamen, inquit, etiamsi superuacuum usum, non turpem nec infamem deo promittunt. Sedent quaedam in Capitolio, quae se a Ioue amari putant: ne Iunonis quidem, si credere poetis uelis, iracundissimae respectu terrentur.[8]

The service these people promise the god, he said, while ineffectual, is not blasphemous or disreputable. Certain women sitting on the Capitol even imagine they are Jupiter's beloved ones. They are not even deterred by fear of Juno, who can be angry in the extreme, if we believe the poets. (tr. J. Rüpke/D. Richardson)

In reproducing the passage I am not motivated, as Augustine was, by a desire to ridicule. It is Seneca in his Stoicism who criticizes the displacement of reason, and calls for moderation in face of emotion.[9] This is indicated by words such as *furor, insanire, dementia*.[10] Like Varro in the century preceding or Valerius Maximus, a few decades earlier, Seneca prefers religious knowledge to emotion.[11] The entire line of argument progresses from supposedly fabricated feelings of loss and joy, governed by

---

[8] Sen. *Superst.* fr. 37 Haase = fr. 70 Vottero (Aug. *Civ.* 6.10).
[9] André 1983, 53.
[10] Even earlier in Sen. *Superst.* fr. 33 Haase = 67 Vottero: ... *taeterrimos hominum affectus* ...
[11] See fr. 43 Haase = 74 Vottero (Aug. *Civ.* 6.11): *Illi* (sc. *Iudaei) tamen causas ritus sui nouerunt. Maior pars populi facit quod cur facit ignorat.* Lausberg 1970, 205–6 has shown that this is referring to the Roman people.

the calendar in the case of Isis (fr. 35), and culminates with being in love with Jupiter. Seneca locates these emotions in sanctuaries. This becomes clear in a rather later fragment cited in the same chapter of Augustine. He, like Seneca, is interested in emotions, but, unlike Seneca, with regard to the gods rather than their temples. The pairing of gods, common to the critiques of both authors,[12] does not relate to mythological pairings, but to cult links, to temples, as is demonstrated by the terms *adoramus* and *cultum*.

If we follow the line of argument indicated by the examples designed to illustrate "superstition", we find intense emotions, and, as I conceive it, a religious experience that transcends social control. In the light of these examples, the temple actually becomes an ambivalent place; it is not just one among many religious locations, but usually a public space, and the most strongly institutionalized and most visible location for religious performance. It is the setting for the least intimate, most traditional, and most closely controlled form of religious activity. This place also shelters the statue of the god, and so provides individuals with the opportunity to experience the gods as being present in their statues; which – so is the judgement – produces the potential for the most scandalous personal behaviour.[13] I shall now turn my attention to this aspect of ancient religion.

A long-term historical perspective

In a European perspective, the critical approach taken by Seneca and Plutarch is not new, and the selection made by Augustine is more than merely typical. The ancient religions that we seek to conceptualize as "traditional religion", "polis religion", "civil cults", or "polytheism as an open system", in order to avoid the generally pejorative term "paganism", were for centuries simply called "idolatry", not only by Jewish and Christian polemicists but also by mere observers.[14] In point of fact, the accommodation of statues in temples was a powerful instrument for ancient religions, enabling the divine to be construed in a differentiated,

---

[12] Sen. *Superst.* fr. 39 Haase = fr. 72 Vottero (Aug. *Civ.* 6.10).

[13] Cf. Sen. *Superst.* fr. 34 Haase = 68 Vottero on the rites of Bellona/Cybele: *se ipsi in templis contrucidant* ...

[14] See F. Schmidt 1987. The speech in Pseudo-Meliton's *Apology*, for instance, is fundamentally addressing ancient paganism as idolatry: "But I, according as I know, will write and shew how and for what causes images were made for kings and tyrants, and they became as gods" (5; Lightfoot 2007, 83).

polytheistic form: or, from another perspective, so represented. The medium of the statue facilitated ritual access, thus practical religious activity; it stimulated reflection, and inspired the imagination in the form of dreams, both sleeping and waking, and visions; it also allowed critical philosophical thinking.[15] The gods could be encountered and addressed in their temples by means of prayers and votive offerings.[16] Sacrifices and the "reading" of entrails facilitated the posing of questions and the receiving of an immediate reply. Inquiries as to the will of the gods in the many forms of divination also frequently referred to this system of representation, as when the statue of a god (usually, however, his or her temple) was struck by a bolt of lightning sent by the god itself, the temple's divine patron, or when the statue turned around or shed blood or tears.[17]

Today, "idolatry" appears to be a less pejorative term. This should at least be the case. In an age of innovation in the public media, images have proved to be a fruitful area for research in the humanities. Specialist disciplines such as art history and iconology have focused research on this theme in the areas of anthropology and the history of religion.[18] Using the concepts and results of such investigations, I shall attempt to provide a rather more precise description of the role of images in Roman religion. I shall ask whether they represent gods, and, if so, how. I hope in this way to clarify the cultural conditions under which behaviour occurred that was criticized as deviant or intellectually aberrant.

Religion with images and without images

In his speech before the pontiffs after his return from exile in 57 BCE, Cicero protested that Clodius had stolen his house without adequate legal justification, in order to transform it into a religious sanctuary: Clodius had consecrated his house, and erected a monument and dedicated a statue on its site (*consecrasse ... monumentum fecisse ... signum dedicasse*).[19] This sequence is an intensification of religious character in linguistic terms. There was no necessary order to the stages themselves.

---

[15] See e.g. Cic. *ND* 1.81.
[16] On an emic reflection of the latter in Propertius 4.2, see Rüpke 2009b.
[17] On the logic see A. Clark 2007, 184–94; in general Rosenberger 1998; Belayche et al. 2005; Belayche and Rüpke 2007; Engels 2007; Annus 2010; Rosenberger 2013a; Santangelo 2013.
[18] Belting 1990; Kippenberg 1990; Stähli 2002; Mitchell 2005; Belting 2007; Lubtchansky and Pouzadoux 2008; Bräunlein 2009; Bredekamp 2010; Mylonopoulos 2010; Faraone 2011; Pezzoli-Olgiati 2011; Dunand 2013.
[19] Cic. *Dom.* 51.

According to Roman property law and normal general practice, a magistrate could dedicate a piece of land to the gods and so transfer possession from the public realm to the realm of divine power, rendering it *sacer*.[20] The second stage in Cicero's argument is that a religious structure need not accommodate a statue, alternatives being an open altar, an enclosure, or a roofed structure. Of course, thirdly, a statue would show unequivocally that such a structure was to be regarded as the "house", *aedes*, of a god, not a storage space or an assembly hall or *schola*: all buildings in which, of course, statues can also be erected. Piety and rituals can also exist without images.

And yet, in Cicero's time, images were important and omnipresent. In the case of Clodius' dubious temple foundation, it was the use of the statue (of which we shall learn more details both in Cicero's discourse and my own) that sealed the sacral nature of the former private house, and removed all remaining ambivalence. Varro, Cicero's contemporary, maintained that the use of statues was an ancient but second-ranking development after 170 years of a cult without images (*deos sine simulacro coluisse*),[21] even though temples – Varro speaks more precisely of roofed structures (*testudines*) – had already been in use in earlier times.[22] Varro refers, probably rightly, to Greek and Etruscan influence in such matters,[23] and also to the fact that sculpture is closely linked with architectural decoration. The truly remarkable innovation was not the one or more statues in temple interiors, but the many on the roof. These remained the distinguishing feature of Etruscan temples and their Roman variants in this and later periods.[24]

I have no intention of disputing the historical exactitude of Varro's philosophically motivated statement postulating the absence of large images somewhere prior to the beginning of the period of monumentalization in the urban context. I fail to see how Varro could have had clear proof of the early absence of images; and yet he was probably right. Only after the most recent research have we been able to date the emergence of anthropomorphic images at both the core and the margin of Middle Eastern and Greek cultures to the end of the first half of the first millennium BCE,

---

[20] See Rüpke 2006b.
[21] Varro, *Ant. rer. div.* fr. 18 Cardauns.
[22] *Serv. auct.*, *Aeneis* 1.505; Cardauns, *comm. ad loc.* 1976, 147. Cf. Varro, *Ant. rer. div.* fr. 70, where *delubrum* refers to images, not *templum*.
[23] Varro, *Ant. rer. div.* fr. 38 Cardauns.
[24] See Cristofani 1987; Zevi 1987; Izzet 2001.

with the exception of Egypt.[25] As already stated, characteristic aspects of Roman religion could function without reference to images. Divine ownership in space and time, in other words consecrated land and *feriae*, feast days marked on the calendar as *NP* and assigned to a single deity,[26] may be seen as a more or less static element. And prayers and sacrifices are feasible without an image to be directly addressed. A makeshift altar of turves and simple clay ware for sacrificial vessels suffice, as Varro stresses in the context of his critique of extravagance in temples.[27] As a description of the late Republican and Imperial ages, however, this is inadequate.

Representation

A Roman of this period did not have to frequent temples in order to know something about images. We must now make a brief diversion through some houses at Pompeii. A visitor to the Casa dei Vettii (VI.15a/b) was met at the entrance by an image of Priapus. This image is particularly celebrated for the fact that the god is weighing his penis against a bag of money on a pair of scales he himself is holding; but it typifies the frequent occurrence of Priapus in entrance contexts. So positioned, the image indicates sexual punishment for thieves and badly behaved guests rather than sexual pleasure.[28] Complex arrangements of doors allowed the doorkeeper to force particular guests into direct confrontation with Priapus, through a smaller entrance, or allow them to avoid the image by using another doorway,[29] only to meet Priapus again in the form of a statue on a fountain in the peristyle.

In a house in area VI.7, famous for the so-called Procession of the Carpenters (showing ordinary people, perhaps the owners, processing with an image of Minerva), a visitor at entrance 9 was greeted with paintings of Mercury and Fortuna to his left and right (now faded). John Clarke's interpretation is supported by many factors: "The owner was, as it were, doubling his luck, since Mercury was the god who made tradesmen and shopkeepers prosper. Fortuna too brought wealth and prosperity." The combination of protective deities was completed outside by an image of Minerva.[30] A third example: a row of four busts showing Sol,

---

[25] See Eich 2011 for Greece; for the ancient Middle East: Ornan 2005, 171. This does not exclude exceptional and short-lived local practices in several places around the Mediterranean and beyond.

[26] See Rüpke 2011b, 126–30.

[27] Varro, *Ant. rer. div.* fr. 38 Cardauns.

[28] Thus e.g. Clarke 1998, 174–7; Balch 2008, 118–19.

[29] Kastenmeier 2001, 307–11.

[30] Clarke 2003, 86.

Jupiter, Mercury, and Luna was set above the entrance to the shop of the "Procession of Cybele" in area IX.7.1. Again I follow Clarke, taking his interpretation further: Sun and Moon locate the shop in a cosmic reference system, in which the bearded Jupiter refers to the Roman polis system, and Mercury to prosperity assured by trade.[31]

As a first attempt at classifying this form of communication between owner and visitor or customer, we might say that it presupposes a standardization of the "medium" and its meaning.[32] A certain number of elements, in this case deities, is combined. Stability of meaning is obtained through iconographic practice.

This mechanism was recognized by Varro. After having systematically described and constructed different groups of highly specialized gods, he added to the fifteen-part structure of his *Antiquitates rerum diuinarum* a sixteenth book, *De dis praecipuis atque selectis* ("On special, selected gods"), defining this new, select group in his introduction as the gods who have been allotted temples and "are distinguished by many signs" (*quibus aedes dedicauerunt eosque pluribus signis ornatos notauerunt*, fr. 228 Cardauns). By the language he uses, Varro appears to be conflating the concept of statues, elsewhere always called *simulacra*, and the attributes that give every statue a unique character. An individual god could be worshipped without an image, as is stressed in fr. 15, but, for further differentiation, temples and images were necessary. Dedication of a statue by women enabled the creation of a Fortuna Muliebris; Fortuna and Felicitas could be distinguished from one another mainly because they had different temples.[33] But this same principle caused Varro problems when it came to imagining how to deal with the many gods already introduced by King Numa. Certainly, Varro might have reasoned, by the time of Numa there had been different rituals (*sacra*) for different gods. But would such essentially transient phenomena have sufficed to distinguish the many gods from one another in a way that would have endured, would have stabilized a complex polytheism without images (and certainly no written texts)? Various circumlocutions and parallel passages suggest that, even though Varro maintains that, in the beginning, there were not yet temples or statues (fr. 38 Cardauns), he nevertheless surmises the existence of smaller forms of sanctuary, or *delubra*.[34]

It must be emphasized that stories, a possible alternative medium, are not mentioned in these contexts. This is not unusual. Considerable

---

[31] Cf. Clarke 2003, 89. Cf. Cic. *Nat.* 1.83: ... *Iouum semper barbatum* ...

[32] The concept of religious communication is examined in Rüpke 2007a, 35–43 and 73–88.

[33] Varro, *Ant. rer. div.* fr. 192 (Muliebris) and 191.

[34] See Varro, *De vita populi Romani* 1, fr. 15 Riposati, and, very explicitly on the problem as to whether one could speak of idolatry before the use of images, Tertullian, *De idolatria* 3.1.

differences between textual and representational codifications of religious knowledge are a frequent phenomenon.[35] The story told by the pontiff Cotta in Cicero's treatise *On the Nature of the Gods* provides important confirmation of this interpretation of the Varro fragments:

> Nobis fortasse sic occurrit, ut dicis; a paruis enim Iouem, Iunonem, Mineruam, Neptunum, Vulcanum, Apollinem, reliquos deos ea facie nouimus, qua pictores fictoresque uoluerunt, neque solum facie, sed etiam ornatu, aetate, uestitu. (1.81)

> What you relate coincides with my own experience. From our youth we have known Jupiter, Juno, Minerva, Neptune, Vulcan, Apollo, and all the other gods only by the particular face given them by painters and sculptors; and not only by that face, but also in their paraphernalia, their age, their dress. (tr. J. Rüpke/D. Richardson)

To the philosophers, this is of course a problem. For such representations are arbitrary and contingent, and not information upon which one can safely establish one's conception of anthropomorphic gods, as Epicureans in fact do.[36] But occasional criticism by intellectuals – shared, of course, by Varro[37] – did not endanger the day-to-day functioning of the semantic system; and intellectuals were also able to contribute something to everyday practice. Varro eventually thought better of his early, critical attitude. Elsewhere, he says that statues and their attributes (*simulacra deorum et insignia ornatusque*) were designed to allow initiates to see the true meaning of the gods, and the world soul (*anima*) to become manifest.[38]

From a historical perspective, other advantages were more important. Iconography's dominance facilitated the creation of new gods; Fortuna Muliebris, "Women's Good Fortune", has already been mentioned. Cults of divine qualities, or of personifications, which appear so strange to modern conceptions of ancient religion, shed all their oddity when considered from a visual perspective. Temples and statues enabled them to become an integral element of the religious system.[39] On the basis of the miracles reported for their temples, Salus, Fortuna, and Concordia – Health, (Good) Fortune, and Harmony – were no different from Juno or Mars. Approximately one-third of reported narratives of miracles relate

---

[35] Stolz 2004, 14 refers to action as a third form of codification of a "religious message" (*religiöse Botschaft*); Uehlinger 2006, 178.

[36] Cic. *Nat.* 1.76–84; cf. Wifstrand Schiebe 2003 on the ontological status of these gods.

[37] See Varro's severe critique, *Ant. rer. div.* fr. 18 Cardauns.

[38] Varro, *Ant. rer. div.* fr. 225 Cardauns.

[39] Clark's (2007) conception of "resources" (among which she also includes festivals) stresses the creative process, and less the psychological effect on recipients.

to temples of such deities.[40] One of the biggest statues of which we possess fragments portrays just such a deity: Fortuna *huiusce diei*. Her statue measured more than 8 metres high. She also stood on a base more than 2 metres high, and must have entirely filled the small chamber of Round Temple B on the Largo Argentina.[41] The process operating here may be described very accurately by the concept of "picturing", popular in recent times: the metaphor of a world being changed by being depicted.[42]

The above observations appear to imply an unrestricted increase in new gods and statues. But the opposite is the case. Cicero's Cotta himself remarks that the number of names of deities in Roman pontifical rituals and texts is in fact limited.[43] An inflation of signs would have imperilled the functioning of the semantic system described above. New cults, if they were to become public, were subjected to a complex procedure of senatorial approval. And Peter Stewart, in his marvellous book on statues in Roman society, has observed how a second possible source of inflation was kept within bounds: "There are strong socio-political pressures that ensure the differentiation of divine and human images in Rome."[44] The conceptual distinction was reflected in the terminology used: "*simulacrum* with its divine associations is specifically *not* applied to honorific and public commemorative statues of human beings".[45] Individual initiative, in the shape, for example, of golden images of C. Iulius Caesar, or so-called private deifications, always threatens the precarious stability of the religion of the elite usually called "public religion".[46]

Images in use

Gradually I return to my starting point: what is praiseworthy and what unacceptable in interactions with images. It is a truism of the "iconic turn"[47] that images arise in the act of seeing, that, through being observed, they are experienced as observing the observer; and that any analysis must give regard to the interaction between object and observer rather than

[40] Clark 2007, 184.
[41] Clark 2007, 128–31.
[42] On the geographical aspect see e.g. Crang 1997.
[43] Cic. *Nat.* 1.84: ... *in pontificiis quidem nostris.*
[44] Stewart 2003, 31.
[45] Stewart 2003, 33. Sylvia Estienne has demonstrated in a lecture at the Max Weber Center at Erfurt that, in this regard, *signum* is used synonymously with *simulacrum* in inscriptions. In Africa in any event, *statua* refers particularly to statues of gods (on synonyms in historiographical literature see Estienne 2010, 259).
[46] See Wrede 1981; Rüpke 2012a, 62–81.
[47] Maar and Burda 2004.

only the qualities inherent to the object, as a semiotic approach does.[48] The temple visitor's gaze changes the image, creating what might be termed a new "social fact". Varro correctly affirms that images of bronze, clay, plaster, or marble[49] have no feelings, do not demand anything, and so evince neither guilt nor gratitude (fr. 22 Cardauns). And yet the supplicant visitor gives the god hearing, even if the deity refuses to grant the wish expressed. Ancient contemporaries themselves provide points of reference for this interpretation in respect of votive practice. We can thus perhaps understand the poem on Vertumnus in the Vicus Tuscus, by the Augustan elegist Propertius, as an analysis of this constructive process.[50]

All this confirms the reverse conclusion at the beginning of my argument. In reflecting on the limits of appropriate religion, one lights upon practices related to statues in the same contexts as criticism of *superstitio*. Even if particular reactions to images, and anthropomorphic images in particular, have an anthropological foundation,[51] such reactions, and even fleeting glances at such images, have a cultural underpinning, and are therefore liable to be the subject of conflicts.

Evidently, many Roman visitors to temples interpreted the confrontation with a statue as a personal encounter. I return to Cicero's speech before the pontiffs. Cicero devotes five paragraphs to the deity to which his house had been dedicated. This speaks for itself (Cic. *Dom.* 108–12):

> Ista tua pulchra Libertas deos penatis et familiaris meos lares expulit, ut se ipsa tamquam in captiuis sedibus conlocaret? ... (110) At quae dea est? Bonam esse oportet, quoniam quidem est abs te dedicata. 'Libertas,' inquit, 'est.' Tu igitur domi meae conlocasti, quam ex urbe tota sustulisti? Tu ... Libertatis simulacrum in ea domo conlocabas, quae domus erat ipsa indicium crudelissimi tui dominatus et miserrimae populi Romani seruitutis? Eumne potissimum Libertas domo sua debuit pellere, qui nisi fuisset in seruorum potestatem ciuitas tota uenisset? (111) At unde est ista inuenta Libertas? quaesiui enim diligenter. Tanagraea quaedam meretrix fuisse dicitur. Eius non longe a Tanagra simulacrum e marmore in sepulcro positum fuit. Hoc quidam homo nobilis, non alienus ab hoc religioso Libertatis sacerdote, ad ornatum aedilitatis suae deportauit ... (112) ... signum de busto meretricis ablatum isti dedit, quod esset signum magis istorum quam publicae libertatis. Hanc deam quisquam uiolare

[48] Briefly Bräunlein 2009, 774–7; Bauer 2007, 105.
[49] Cf. Seneca, *Superstitiones* fr. 31 Haase = fr. 65 Vottero (Aug. *Civ.* 6.10) on the conflict between the invulnerability of the gods and the unworthiness of the object.
[50] Prop. 4.2; see Rüpke 2009b.
[51] Mitchell 2005; Bredekamp 2010.

audeat, imaginem meretricis, ornamentum sepulcri, a fure sublatam, a sacrilego conlocatam? haec me domo mea pellet? haec uictrix adflictae ciuitatis rei publicae spoliis ornabitur? haec erit in eo monumento quod positum est ut esset indicium oppressi senatus ad memoriam sempiternae turpitudinis?

This, your splendid Libertas, has driven out my Penates, the Lares of my family, so that she herself can straightaway settle as if on a conquered place? … (110) But what kind of a deity is that? It must be a "good" one [Clodius owed his notoriety to the scandal concerning Bona Dea], as you yourself dedicated it. "No," he says, "this is 'Liberty'!" So have you set up in my house the goddess that you removed from the entire city? … you set the image of Liberty in the very house that has become a symbol of your most cruel tyranny, and of the most abject slavery of the Roman people? Did Liberty have to drive from his house the very man whose actions alone had prevented the entire citizenry from coming under the control of slaves? (111) And where was this particular Liberty discovered? I have investigated this thoroughly! It is said she was a whore from Tanagra. Her marble image stood on her grave not far from Tanagra. A nobleman, not unknown to this scrupulous priest of Liberty, took this image as decoration for his term as *aedile* … (112) … he gave the image removed from the whore's pyre to that man so that it should serve as an image of the liberty of such men in place of public liberty. This goddess, who would dare to impugn her, this representation of a whore, this funeral ornament, carried off by a thief, and erected by a desecrator of temples? Is she to drive me from my house? Is she to be adorned as victor over the assailed citizenry with the spoils of war that rightly belong to us all? Is she to stand in the monument that has been set up as an eternal reminder of the suppression of the Senate? (tr. D. Richardson/J. Rüpke)

The passage begins and ends with personifications. Libertas, the goddess "Liberty", is an active entity driving Cicero from his house. He recounts the history of the actual statue, how it came from a prostitute's grave and then was subject to a series of illicit removals. But Cicero does not distinguish between the goddess and her material manifestation. *Ista tua Libertas*, "your particular type of liberty", is no benevolent address to a goddess. It is perverse that the arch-enemy of liberty should turn to such a deity. But it is nevertheless a deity. Semantically and syntactically, the conceptual and material forms of the deity are treated with strict equivalence, and stress is placed on the identity of the two forms: *at quae dea est* (110) parallels *at unde est* (111). The goddess is present in her *simulacrum*, "statue", and it is in the form of a *simulacrum* that she acts. *Libertatis simulacrum in ea domo* … (110) parallels *Libertas domo sua* … (111). The goddess is as negative as her statue, and vice versa.

This conception of presence is reflected in archaeological discoveries made by Henner von Hesberg and Dirk Steuernagel. In parallel with a development manifested in the restoration of some Greek temples from the Hellenistic and Imperial ages,[52] although predominantly in Sicily and Southern Italy, Roman temples appear to have stage-managed this sense of presence to create an appropriate experience for the temple visitor. Indicators for this are the lavish interiors of the temples,[53] complex architectural manipulation of temple access, and very careful presentation of the cult statue. Increased importance was given to doorways and entrances; floor mosaics or curtains might be used to structure the interior as well as the time involved in entering the temple.[54] Positioning a statue without articulated base directly on the mosaic floor might emphasize its mobility, as if the gaze of the visitor just catches the god in movement.[55] Combining different materials might heighten the lifelike impression.[56] This does not fit well with the Greek tradition of an aesthetic that commanded reverence by means of a fine, substantial image at the rear wall of the innermost chamber.[57]

The anecdotal evidence referred to earlier confirms observations made so far. It was said that P. Cornelius Scipio Africanus spent every night before a momentous decision sitting in the *cella* of Jupiter in the Capitoline Temple, often alone, as if he were conducting a dialogue with the god (*quasi consultantem de republica cum Ioue*).[58]

But such experiences with the god were not confined to individual visitors to the temple. Temples might be robbed or destroyed, which was a sacrilege. But temples and statues were often also attacked by the gods themselves, in a form of *prodigium* or portent.[59] What was happening in those instances? In mythological vein in his poem on his own consulate, Cicero imagines Jupiter hurling down lightning bolts on his own temple, and thus clearly distinguishes the god from the god's image.[60] The Epicurean Lucretius (died about 55 BCE) referred to this phenomenon

---

[52] Steuernagel 2009, 124–6.
[53] Steuernagel 2009, 124–6.
[54] Hesberg 2007. According to Pliny (*HN* 36.185), mosaics were installed in the Capitoline temple of Jupiter in 149 BCE.
[55] Hesberg 2007, 458–9.
[56] Hesberg 2007, 456.
[57] See Bäbler and Nesselrath 2006, 141. For the aesthetics of colossal statues see Cancik 2003, 224–48.
[58] Gell. *NA* 6.1.6; Liv. 26.19.5 (*consideret*); see Rüpke 2007b, 13.
[59] In general Rosenberger 1998; see also his critique of MacBain in Rosenberger 2005 (not taken into account by Engels 2008, 753–4).
[60] Cic. fr. 10. 36–8 Courtney = Cic. *Div.* 1.19; criticized in 2.45–7.

as an argument against the divine origin of lightning.[61] Both writers go against standard practice in concentrating on Jupiter. Religious specialists were regularly called upon to interpret declared prodigies, and it was taken as read that it was the god of the temple concerned, or his statue, to which one must turn after such a portent, be it the sudden appearance of a wolf or the destructive power of a storm or of lightning.[62]

This interpretation had practical consequences when, in 208 BCE, the pontiffs pronounced against the dedication of a common temple *cella* for two gods, Honos and Virtus. They argued that, in the event of a portent, they would no longer be able to determine with any certainty the recipient of the required ritual.[63] There is no theorizing in those passages describing the *prodigium* or the subsequent rituals, nothing resembling Plutarch's concession that, thinking of weeping statues, a god could indicate something by natural processes.[64] Whatever may have been the cause or circumstances of the foundation of a temple or dedication of a statue to a particular deity, either in the case of age-old deities with many stories that could be told, or in that of newly deified qualities,[65] miracles maintained the deity's presence, and demonstrated that it was involved in Roman affairs: not from just anywhere, but from that one particular location, and in the form given him or her in religious representation.

Presence and representation

In what terms can we best couch our findings? The idea of representation is my suggested starting point,[66] and is eminently useful if priority is first given to the notion of the metaphysical existence of the gods. The statue is a sign or symbol for something else; it makes visible the invisible.[67] Such an interpretation is reconcilable with ancient philosophical

---

[61] Lucr. 6.417–19.
[62] Rosenberger 1998, 64.
[63] Liv. 27.25.7–9: *Marcellum aliae atque aliae obiectae animo religiones tenebant, in quibus quod cum bello Gallico ad Clastidium aedem Honori et Virtuti uouisset dedicatio eius a pontificibus impediebatur, (8) quod negabant unam cellam amplius quam uni deo recte dedicari, quia si de caelo tacta aut prodigii aliquid in ea factum esset difficilis procuratio foret, quod utri deo res diuina fieret sciri non posset; (9) neque enim duobus nisi certis deis rite una hostia fieri. ita addita Uirtutis aedes adproperato opere; neque tamen ab ipso aedes eae dedicatae sunt.* Cf. Rüpke 1995, 492–3 on the translation of *expiatio* avoided by me.
[64] Plut. *Coriol.* 38, cited in Rosenberger 1998, 26–7.
[65] See Clark 2007, 190–1.
[66] Rüpke 2007a, 53–69, and 2009b.
[67] See Lubtchansky and Pouzadoux 2008.

and theological thinking. It is possible to discuss the suitability and appropriateness of the semiotic material, in the sense both of metaphor[68] and of actual objects: this was a real political discourse in respect of statues of emperors, beginning with Caesar.[69]

The normal indexicality of signs brings with it an advantage that has already been emphasized by Hans-Georg Gadamer, whose position may be summarized as follows: "Every representation reinforces the onto-logical reality of the object represented."[70] Or, more aptly: if images relate to gods, then gods must exist. Discussions may ensue as to the iconicity, the verisimilitude of the sign, as we have seen in the imagined argument between the Epicurean Velleius and the Sceptic Cotta in Cicero's dialogue *De natura deorum*.

"Representation" does not work well as a description for the Roman attitude, which we have considered with reference to widespread practice; no more does "transitory presence". As Richard Gordon has shown so well in respect of Greek religion,[71] the possibility of affirming or denying a god's presence when one is standing before his or her image does not work by means of conceptions of "inhabiting" or "finding a transitory location",[72] which are all predicated on a metaphysical distinction between god and image. But it would be naive just to opt for "presence",[73] even if we were to confine ourselves to a kind of mainstream observer. Roman gods were not simply present in their images. In contrast to Varro, neither Seneca nor Plutarch either denies or affirms their presence.[74] On the contrary, they criticize images as such very vividly.

As regards Roman images other than statues, it may be said that they are often not realistic, and make no attempt to give a fully "lifelike" representation of the deity. Instead, these images themselves actually relate to statues. They are representations of statues, and categorized as such iconographically. Peter Stewart has shown that this is the case in different genres.

---

[68] See Ando 2001 for Augustine's consideration of and quarrel with earlier traditions, and Wallraff 2003.

[69] See e.g. Cass. Dio 43.45 on statues of Caesar, and Plin. *Pan.* 52.3 (Plin. *HN* 34.15–16 attests to the Republic's oldest statue made of gold).

[70] Ouwerkerk 1987, 161. This is a stronger idea than Clifford Geertz's "aura of facticity" (Geertz 1966, 1), derived from specifically religious material.

[71] Gordon 1979. See also Gladigow 2005, 62–84.

[72] Cf. Steiner 2001, 79: container, vessel, residence.

[73] Cf. Hubbeling 1986.

[74] Cf. Moellering 1963, 117–18 for incoherences in Plutarch's theology of images. With particular reference to the dialogue *De E apud Delphos* (393D), Baldassarri 1996, 386–7 has pointed to Plutarch's fideistic proclivities.

Roman coins often provide a (non-realistic) view into a temple, of something resembling a statue or of a living god.[75] Lamps give frontal views of gods (and humans) in the form of a statue.[76] Idyllic landscape murals depict statues of gods, revealing the divine presence to the painted images of visitors.[77] The presence of the gods is not arbitrary, but it takes the form of statues. This presence does not acquire its plausibility from a specific form or material, but from an emotional experience arising from the specific context of the temple, sometimes reinforced by ritual,[78] sometimes by the god's proven ability, for instance to heal.[79] The many gods of Roman polytheism acquired existence through representation, and through human experience of their statues. Birgit Meyer has suggested the concept of " 'sensational forms' that trigger as well as condense religious experience"; this captures the mechanism to be observed in the Roman context very well.[80]

The lesson thus learned is important for the reading of cult scenes such as those with which I began. The wall painting of the Cybele procession on the outside wall of a shop with the same name (IX.7.1) does not merely represent (presumably) the shop owner and his wife (with other colleagues) together with some spectators. Cybele is in the picture, unmistakably characterized as a seated statue in a litter, but double life-size; in a real sense, she is meeting all the people who are looking at her. We are not in a position to repeat the experience of the original observers; we do not share their religious individuation. But we can try to imagine their prior experiences and habits, their internal image world, their cultural posture.[81] In this way, we may find a reference to a presence that, while not anthropologically inherent to the image, belongs to it by virtue of historical circumstances[82] that I have attempted to reconstruct.

Summary: experience

Despite the centrality of experience in thinking about religion since the end of the eighteenth century, the term has not been used in respect of ancient religion outside Judaism and Christianity, apart from a small

[75] Stewart 2003, 208–14.
[76] Stewart 2003, 207.
[77] Hesberg 2004, 214–15; cf. Stewart 2003, 215–21.
[78] For this factor, which I have not used here, Versnel 1987.
[79] See Graf 2001, 242.
[80] Meyer 2008, 129.
[81] Kramer 2001.
[82] For the post-antique history of statues in Europe, see e.g. Beutler 1982; Stuckrad 2006.

number of comparatively recent book titles.[83] The very subjectivity of "experience" (*pathos*,[84] unlike the ancient idea of *experientia*, or learning by doing) appears to come up short against the lack of ancient sources. Recent analyses have nevertheless developed a concept of experience that takes account of the link between personal experience and communicated meaning, and opens a perspective for historical application. "Personal, lived experience in its qualitatively emotional dimension, so long as it is not articulated symbolically, remains silent, and unable to alter behaviour." Conversely, in the opinion of Matthias Jung, "any system of convictions and practices that is no longer capable of expressing qualitative experiences from a first-person standpoint becomes progressively obsolete".[85] Accordingly, by concentrating on "experience" in the context of our religious-historical investigations we are able to focus on the actor, the observer and user of images and of the sacral space, the person who moves in that space, or towards it in the context of pilgrimage.[86]

The "superstition" perspective on the potentially dangerous role of sanctuaries in religion, as illustrated by two intellectuals from the first century CE, was not the only voice to be heard. Others were able to develop a more positive view. For the Imperial age, perhaps as early as the Augustan age, Hero of Alexandria describes a whole selection of instruments and mechanisms designed to contrive with the aid of mirrors an emotionally intense and startling confrontation with the god in the temple.[87] The following mechanisms are described in his *Pneumatica*: set around an altar, figures that move and perform libations as soon as incense is burned at the altar (1.12); a trumpet that sounds when the temple doors are opened (1.17); in a rite peculiar to Egyptian temples, water running over moving oars (1.32); temple doors that open and close in a variety of technical modes when a fire is lit and extinguished on an altar positioned opposite the temple (1.38–9). The second book describes a transparent altar of glass or horn, within which figures move as soon as the fire is lit (2.3). Lastly, a still more complex arrangement is mentioned, with figures performing a libation, and a hissing snake coiled around an altar (2.21). It must

---

[83] Bispham and Smith 2000; Cole 2004. "Emotionality" has been given more attention, but must not be related to individuality: Linke 2003, 84.

[84] At the Boston SBL conference in 2008, Troels Engberg-Pedersen presented an attempt to define and identify religious experience by means of this term.

[85] Jung 2006, 21; see also Jung 2004 and Schlette and Jung 2005, especially Jung 2005.

[86] See e.g. Petsalis-Diomidis 2005.

[87] I am grateful to Mihaela Holban, Erfurt, for referring me to this text.

be stressed that, contrary to our experience of modern apparatuses from former centuries, no theatre is shown in respect of the device described in Hero's *Automatopoiêtikê*, but, instead, a ritual scene around an altar in front of a temple. This should remind us that, even without mechanical aids, architectural contrivances could provide an intense experience.

The cry of "Superstition!" is a possible reaction, but not a necessary one. That cry is very helpful to us, as the search by contemporaries for deviance helps us to identify the dynamic elements of traditionally based ancient religion. Its overall definition remains open. It could be understood either as a discourse in progress or as a mere incoherent babble of voices that in the first century remained without consequences.[88] Along with Richard Gordon, I tend to see in the segment described so far an elite discourse, an attempt to purify traditional religion from a theoretical point of view, resulting in an attempt at popularizing aristocratic behaviour. The figures criticized in the process still remained virtually untouched in their actual behaviour by this discourse. But things might change.

---

[88] Even Plutarch describes a positive, joyful effect on the occasion of festivals in temples (*Non posse sua uita uiui secundum Epicurum*, 1101E, see Moreschini 1996, 45–8).

CHAPTER 5

The normative discourse in Late Antiquity

What was regulated?

Having examined the texts of the first century CE devoted to *superstitio* and *deisidaimonia*, I shall turn my attention in this chapter to a quite different genre: that of legal texts. How did Imperial age legal texts address religious transgressions? How does "religion" feature in the great collections of statutes? What can lists of rules and prohibitions tell us that is of relevance to the question of religious deviance and the leeway enjoyed by individuals in respect of their religious activity? Before turning to the Late Antique collections of legal texts, I should like to indicate two categories that will play no further role in what follows.

It can come as no surprise, in the light of the questions posed above, that the first of those categories concerns magic and legal measures to combat it. A dissertation that appeared in 2003 bears the title *Religio et sacrilegium: Studies on the Criminalization of Magic, Heresy, and Paganism (4th–7th Centuries)*.[1] But the link alluded to is not a matter of simple self-evidence. The editors of the *Codex Theodosianus*, in the final volume of this collection of norms from the fourth and fifth centuries pertaining to the religious sphere, and ranging from rightful belief and bishops to heretics and pagans (Book 16), did not concern themselves with magical practices. The criminalization of felonies such as murder by poisoning is not pursued in religious terms, even though, phenomenologically, a propinquity to other magical practices or even an identity of actors may commonly have been assumed: or rather, in the context of literary texts, assumed. The Severan jurist Ulpian, in Book 7 of his work on provincial administration (*De officio proconsulis*), writes "on mathematicians and soothsayers" in purely non-religious terms: punishment should be apportioned solely "on the basis of answers given when questioned", and

---

[1] Zeddies 2003; magic and superstition are similarly treated as synonymous in Bailey 2007.

according to the content and purposes of the particular inquiry into present and future events.[2] Murder by poisoning is missing from Cicero's list of religious offences concluding the second book of his *Laws*.

To clarify: the above findings are purely textually based. They concern the semantics of legal texts, not their pragmatics. I do not wish to deny that laws against causing bodily injury by magic were used to penalize religious practices.[3] But such penalization was directed against concrete offences: Apuleius was not arraigned for magical activities in the abstract, but for fraudulently obtaining a marriage by means of nocturnal acts of sacrifice (*nocturna sacra*, Apul. *Apol.* 57.2), thereby winning the hand of the older, wealthy Pudentilla. Apuleius was accused of the murder of his brother-in-law Pontianus, of grave *magica maleficia*, "magical misdeeds" (1), and – as he states in his final plea – bodily injury by *ueneficia*, the preparation of poison (102). The time of day is of course indicative of evil intent. Cicero too had expressed distrust of nocturnal rituals (Cic. *Leg.* 2.2). Apuleius' plea accordingly includes a denial of the material facts (Apul. *Apol.* 58 ff.). He questions the credibility of the witness. Before the era of scientific evidence, poisonings did not differ from assaults by means of curses: the victim bore no wounds. Any action at all might be adjudged to have been causal. Apuleius' defence is aimed at rendering plausible his role as philosopher. Religion does not enter into it.

My second point concerns legislation on colleges. Roman law on associations was ancient.[4] It was traced back to Numa, who was supposed to have authorized trade associations and founded priestly colleges. Not until Caesar and Augustus, however, with their respective specific laws *de collegiis*, does there appear to have existed a legal description of "associations".[5] The Imperial age too failed to create a strict legal framework. The tradition is marked by politically opportunistic rules, isolated decisions in respect of individual cases, and what appears to have been a quite heterogeneous practice in respect of the statutory creation and oversight of associations.[6]

All this had nothing to do with the law of religion. Groups of religious functionaries (*sacerdotes*, *symphoniaci*) or local groups of worshippers (*cultores*) of a god would doubtless also, in particular cases, aspire to the

[2] *Collatio legum Romanarum et Mosaicarum* 15.2.
[3] On the problem of magic, see Philipps 1991, 1994; Kippenberg 1997; Zeddies 2003; a full treatment in Otto 2011.
[4] Kippenberg 2005, 42–4.
[5] Bendlin 2005, 92–3.
[6] Bendlin 2005, 96–104.

mutual ties associated with the status of a *collegium*.[7] In terms of the law, the *collegium* or *corpus* was important as a corporate body alongside political association or *ciuitas*: as a potential holder of property rights capable, by virtue of its status as a legal person, to interact on the same level as other, "natural" persons.[8] Unlike the family, which was seen as a natural social form, these forms of association also drew importance from their ability to enter into free contractual obligations with one another. Such obligations also applied in the public realm,[9] and thus mutual bonds were formed between the institutions in question.[10] Constantine, in a law of 321, understood the Church as an association in order to ensure that legacies to it retained their validity:

> Habeat uniuscuiusque licentiam sanctissimae catholicae uenerabilique concilio decedens bonorum quod optauit relinquere.

> Everyone, at his death, shall have the capacity to bequeath whatever goods he wishes to the most holy, all-embracing, and worshipful assembly. (tr. D. Richardson/J. Rüpke)

Whether Constantine is here thinking of more than only the Church in the city of Rome, to which he himself assigned land and buildings in abundance, is unclear.[11] Already in 313, however, not only had individual Christians been granted freedom of religion by the so-called Edict of Milan, but their local organizations (*conuenticula*) too, as well as a supra-regional body (*corpus*), had been recognized as potential holders of property and recipients of restitution. The text is to be found in Lactantius (*On the Deaths of the Persecutors* 48.1–11), and I quote it here in full because of its general significance in terms of the history of religion. It is introduced in a letter sent by Licinius after his arrival in Nicomedia:

> (2) Cum feliciter tam ego [quam] Constantinus Augustus quam etiam ego Licinius Augustus apud Mediolanum conuenissemus atque uniuersa quae ad commoda et securitatem publicam pertinerent, in tractatu haberemus, haec inter cetera quae uidebamus pluribus hominibus profutura, uel in primis ordinanda esse credidimus, quibus diuinitatis reuerentia continebatur, ut daremus et Christianis et omnibus liberam potestatem sequendi religionem quam quisque uoluisset, quod quicquid <est> diuinitatis in

---

[7] E.g. *CIL* 6.2193 = *ILS* 4966; *CIL* 14.2112.10–13 = *ILS* 7212.

[8] See Gai. *Dig.* 3.4.1.1.

[9] Stressed by Kippenberg 2009, 130.

[10] Bendlin 2005, 74–5.

[11] The question of the date from which Constantine understood "catholic" as the mere claim of rival churches must remain open (Clark 2005, 96).

sede caelesti. Nobis atque omnibus qui sub potestate nostra sunt constituti, placatum ac propitium possit existere. (3) Itaque hoc consilium salubri ac reticissima ratione ineundum esse credidimus, ut nulli omnino facultatem abnegendam putaremus, qui vel obseruationi Christianorum uel ei religioni mentem suam dederet quam ipse sibi aptissimam esse sentiret, ut possit nobis summa diuinitas, cuius religioni liberis mentibus obsequimur, in omnibus solitum fauorem suum beniuolentiamque praestare. (4) Quare scire dicationem tuam conuenit placuisse nobis, ut amotis omnibus omnino condicionibus quae prius scriptis ad officium tuum datis super Christianorum nomine <continebantur, et quae prorsus sinistra et a nostra clementia aliena esse> uidebantur, <ea remoueantur. Et> nunc libere ac simpliciter unus quisque eorum, qui eandem obseruandae religionis Christianorum gerunt uoluntatem. Citra ullam inquietudinem ac molestiam sui id ipsum obseruare contendant. (5) Quae sollicitudini tuae plenissime significanda esse credidimus, quo scires nos liberam atque absolutam colendae religionis suae facultatem isdem Christianis dedisse. (6) Quod cum isdem a nobis indultum esse peruideas, intellegit dicatio tua etiam aliis religionis suae uel obseruantiae potestatem similiter apertam et liberam pro quiete temporis nostri <esse> concessam, ut in colendo quod quisque delegerit, habeat liberam facultatem. <Quod a nobis factum est. Ut neque cuiquam> honori neque cuiquam religioni detractum aliquid a nobis <uideatur>.

(7) Atque hoc insuper in persona Christianorum statuendum esse censuimus, quod, si eadem loca, ad quae antea conuenire consuerant, de quibus etiam datis ad officium tuum litteris certa antehac forma fuerat comprehensa. Priore tempore aliqui uel a fisco nostro uel ab alio quocumque uidentur esse mercati, eadem Christianis sine pecunia et sine ulla pretii petitione, postposita omni frustratione atque ambiguitate restituant; qui etiam dono fuerunt consecuti, eadem similiter isdem Christianis quantocius reddant, etiam uel hi qui emerunt uel qui dono fuerunt consecuti, si petiuerint de nostra beniuolentia aliquid, uicarium postulent, quo et ipsis per nostram clementiam consulatur. Quae omnia corpori Christianorum protinus per intercessionem tuam ac sine mora tradi oportebit. (8) Et quoniam idem Christiani non [in] ea loca tantum ad quae conuenire consuerunt, sed alia etiam habuisse noscuntur ad ius corporis eorum id est ecclesiarum, non hominum singulorum, pertinentia, ea omnia lege quam superius comprehendimus, citra ullam prorsus ambiguitatem uel controuersiam isdem Christianis id est corpori et conuenticulis eorum reddi iubebis, supra dicta scilicet ratione seruata, ut ii qui eadem sine pretio sicut diximus restituant, indemnitatem de nostra beniuolentia sperent.

(9) In quibus omnibus supra dicto corpori Christianorum intercessionem tuam efficacissimam exhibere debebis, ut praeceptum nostrum quantocius compleatur, quo etiam in hoc per clementiam nostram quieti publicae consulatur. (10) Hactenus fiet, ut, sicut superius comprehensum est, diuinus iuxta nos favor, quem in tantis sumus rebus experti, per

omne tempus prospere successibus nostris cum beatitudine publica perseue-
eret. (11) Ut autem huius sanctionis <et> beniuolentiae nostrae forma ad
omnium possit peruenire notitiam, prolata programmate tuo haec scripta
et ubique proponere et ad omnium scientiam te perferre conueniet, ut
huius nostrae beniuolentiae [nostrae] sanctio latere non possit.

When I, Constantine Augustus, and I, Licinius Augustus, happily met
at Milan and had under consideration all matters which concerned the
public advantage and safety, we thought that, among all the other things
that we saw would benefit the majority of men, the arrangements which
above all needed to be made were those which ensured reverence for the
Divinity, so that we might grant both to Christians and to all men freedom to follow whatever religion each one wished, in order that whatever
divinity there is in the seat of heaven may be appeased and made propitious towards us and towards all who have been set under our power.
We thought therefore that in accordance with salutary and most correct
reasoning we ought to follow the policy of regarding this opportunity
as one not to be denied to anyone at all, whether he wished to give his
mind to the observances of the Christians or to that religion which he felt
was most fitting to himself, so that the supreme Divinity, whose religion
we obey with free minds, may be able to show in all matters His accustomed favour and benevolence towards us. For this reason we wish your
Devotedness to know that we have resolved that, all the conditions which
were contained in letters previously sent to your office about the Christian
name being completely set aside, those measures should be repealed which
seemed utterly inauspicious and foreign to our clemency, and that each
individual one of those who share this same wish to observe the religion
of the Christians should freely and straightforwardly hasten to do so without any anxiety or interference. We thought that this should be very fully
communicated to your Solicitude, so that you should know that we have
given a free and absolute permission to these same Christians to practise their religion. And when you perceive that this indulgence has been
accorded by us to these people, your Devotedness understands that others
too have been granted a similarly open and free permission to follow their
own religion and worship as befits the peacefulness of our times, so that
each man may have a free opportunity to engage in whatever worship he
has chosen. This we have done to ensure that no cult or religion may seem
to have been impaired by us.

We have also decided that we should decree as follows about the
Christians as a body; if, during the period that has passed, any appear to
have purchased either from our treasury or from anyone else those places
in which the Christians had previously been accustomed to assemble,
and about which before now a definite rule had been laid down in the
letters that were sent to your office, they should now restore these same
places to the Christians without receiving any money for them or making any request for payment, and without any question of obstruction or

equivocation; those who received such places as a gift should return them in the same way but the more speedily to these same Christians; both those who bought them, and those who received them as gifts should, if they seek something from our benevolence make a request of the deputy for their interests to be consulted by our clemency. All these places must forth-with be handed over to the body of the Christians through your interven-tion and without any delay.

And since these same Christians are known to have possessed not only the places in which they had the habit of assembling but other property too which belongs by right to their body – that is, to the churches not to individuals – you will order all this property, in accordance with the law which we have explained above, to be given back without any equivocation or dispute at all to these same Christians, that is to their body and assem-blies, preserving always the principle stated above, that those who restore this same property as we have enjoined without receiving a price for it may hope to secure indemnity from our benevolence. In all these matters you will be bound to offer the aforesaid body of Christians your most effective support so that our instructions can be the more rapidly carried out and the interest of public tranquility thereby served in this matter too by our clemency. In this way it will come about, as we have explained above, that the divine favour towards us, which we have experienced in such important matters, will continue for all time to prosper our achievements along with the public well-being. (tr. J. Creed, Oxford, 1984)

Here, colleges are not seen as a distinct social form of religion. Although Tertullian, describing Christianity a good hundred years previously in his *Apology*, referred to the law in respect of associations, his concern was not to prove conformity with Roman legal norms.[12] Arguing from the spirit of the law concerning associations, which prohibited the formation of par-ties (*factiones*) on the grounds that they might disturb the public peace (38–9), he proposed that the correct term in respect of Christianity might be "council for the public good" (*curia*) rather than "party" (39.21). I cite this text too in substantial part, as it comprehensively sets out the prob-lems at issue at the turn of the second century:

(38.1) Proinde nec paulo lenius inter <il>licitas factiones sectam istam deputari oportebat, a qua nihil tale committitur, quale de illicitis factioni-bus timeri solet. (2) Nisi fallor enim, prohibendarum factionum causa de prouidentia constat modestiae publicae, ne ciuitas in partes scinderetur, quae res facile comitia concilia curias contiones, spectacula etiam aemu-lis studiorum compulsationibus inquietaret, cum iam et in quaestu habere

¹² Interpretation of the passage from Tertullian is disputed; cf. Bendlin 2005, Kippenberg 2005, 52–3; 102–3; Kippenberg 2009, 136–8.

coepissent uenalem et mercenariam homines uiolentiae suae operam. (3) At enim nobis ab omni gloriae et dignitatis ardore frigentibus nulla est necessitas coetus nec ulla magis res aliena quam publica. Unam omnium rem publicam agnoscimus, mundum …

(39.1) Edam iam nunc ego ipse negotia Christianae factionis, ut, qui mala refutauerim, bona ostendam. Corpus sumus de conscientia religionis et disciplinae unitate et spei foedere. (2) Coimus in coetum et congregationem, ut ad deum quasi manu facta precationibus ambiamus orantes. Haec uis deo grata est. Oramus etiam pro imperatoribus, pro ministris eorum et potestatibus, pro statu saeculi, pro rerum quiete, pro mora finis. (3) Coimus ad litterarum diuinarum commemorationem, si quid praesentium temporum qualitas aut praemonere cogit aut recognoscere. Certe fidem sanctis uocibus pascimus, spem erigimus, fiduciam figimus, disciplinam praeceptorum nihilominus inculcationibus densamus. (4) Ibidem etiam exhortationes, castigationes et censura diuina. Nam et iudicatur magno cum pondere, ut apud certos de dei conspectu, summumque futuri iudicii praeiudicium est, si quis ita deliquerit, ut a communicatione orationis et conuentus et omnis sancti commercii relegetur. (5) Praesident probati quique seniores, honorem istum non pretio, sed testimonio adepti, neque enim pretio ulla res dei constat. Etiam, si quod arcae genus est, non de honoraria summa quasi redemptae religionis congregatur. Modicam unusquisque stipem menstrua die, uel cum uelit et si modo uelit et si modo possit, apponit. Nam nemo compellitur, sed sponte confert. (6) Haec quasi deposita pietatis sunt. Nam inde non epulis nec potaculis nec ingratis uoratrinis dispensatur, sed egenis alendis humandisque et pueris ac puellis re ac parentibus destitutis iamque domesticis senibus, item naufragis et si qui in metallis et si qui in insulis uel in custodiis, dumtaxat ex causa dei sectae, alumni confessionis suae fiunt. (7) Sed eiusmodi uel maxime dilectionis operatio notam nobis inurit penes quosdam. "Vide", inquiunt, "ut inuicem se diligant" – ipsi enim inuicem oderunt – "et ut pro alterutro mori sint parati"; ipsi enim ad occidendum alterutrum paratiores erunt. (8) Sed et quod fratres nos uocamus, non alias, opinor, insaniunt, quam quod apud ipsos omne sanguinis nomen de affectione simulatum est. Fratres autem etiam uestri sumus iure naturae matris unius, etsi uos parum homines, quia mali fratres. (9) At quanto dignius fratres et dicuntur et habentur, qui unum patrem deum agnouerint, qui unum spiritum biberint sanctitatis, qui de uno utero ignorantiae eiusdem ad unam lucem expauerint ueritatis! (10) Sed eo fortasse minus legitimi existimamur, quia nulla de nostra fraternitate tragoedia exclamat, uel quia ex substantia familiari fratres sumus, quae penes uos fere dirimit fraternitatem.

(11) Itaque qui animo animaque miscemur, nihil de rei communicatione dubitamus. Omnia indiscreta sunt apud nos praeter uxores …

(16) Cena nostra de nomine rationem sui ostendit: Id uocatur quod dilectio penes Graecos. Quantiscumque sumptibus constet, lucrum est pietatis nomine facere sumptum, siquidem inopes quosque refrigerio isto

iuuamus, non qua penes uos parasiti affectant ad gloriam famulandae
libertatis sub auctoramento uentris inter contumelias saginandi, sed qua
penes deum maior est contemplatio mediocrium. (17) Si honesta causa
est conuiuii, reliquum ordinem disciplinae de causa aestimate! Quod sit
de religionis officio, nihil uilitatis, nihil immodestiae admittit. Non prius
discumbitur quam oratio ad deum praegustetur; editur quantum esuri-
entes capiunt; bibitur quantum pudicis utile est. (18) Ita saturantur, ut
qui meminerint, etiam per noctem adorandum deum sibi esse; ita fabu-
lantur, ut qui sciant dominum audire. Post aquam manualem et lumina,
ut quisque de scripturis sanctis uel de proprio ingenio potest, prouoca-
tur in medium deo canere; hinc probatur quomodo biberit. Aeque oratio
conuiuium dirimit. (19) Inde disceditur non in cateruas caesionum nec
in classes discursationum nec in eruptiones lasciuiarum, sed ad eandem
curam modestiae et pudicitiae, ut qui non tam cenam cenauerint quam
disciplinam.

(20) Haec coitio Christianorum merito sane illicita, si illicitis par, merito damnanda, si quis de ea queritur eo titulo, quo de factionibus querela
est. (21) In cuius perniciem aliquando conuenimus? Hoc sumus congre-
gati, quod et dispersi, hoc uniuersi, quod et singuli: Neminem laedentes,
neminem contristantes. Cum probi, cum boni coeunt, cum pii, cum casti
congregantur, non est factio dicenda, sed curia.

(38.1) Was not a rather gentler treatment in order? When it commits no
such actions as are commonly feared from unlawful associations? (2) For,
unless I am mistaken, the reason for prohibiting associations clearly lay
in forethought for public order – to save the State from being torn into
parties, a thing very likely to disturb election assemblies, public gatherings, local incentives, meetings, even the public games with the clashing
and rivalry of partisans, especially since men had begun to reckon on their
violence as a source of revenue, offering it for sale at the price. (3) We, however, whom all the flames of glory and dignity leave cold, have no need to
confine; nothing is more foreign to us than the State. One state we know,
of which all citizens – the universe …

(39.1) I will now show you the proceedings with which the Christian
Association occupies itself; I have proof that they are not wrong; so now
I really make you see they are good. We are society with a common religious feelings, unity of discipline, the common bond of hope. (2) We meet
in gathering and congregation to approach God in prayer, massing our
forces to surround Him. This violence that we do him pleases God. We
pray also for Emperors, for their ministers and those in authority, for the
security of the world, for peace on earth, for postponement of the end.
(3) We meet to read the books of God – if anything in the nature of the
times bids us look to the future or open our eyes to facts. In any case, with
those holy words we feed our faith, we lift up our hope, we confirm our
confidence; and no less we reinforce our teaching by inculcation of God's
precepts. There is, besides, exhortation in our gatherings, rebuke, divine

censure. (4) For judgement is passed, and it carries great weight, as it must among men certain that God sees them; and it is a notable foretaste of judgement to come, if any man has so sinned as to be banished from all share in our prayer, our assembly, and all holy intercourse. (5) Our presidents are elders of proved character, men who have reached this honour not for a price, but by character; for nothing that is God's goes for a price.

Even if there is a chest of a sort, it is not made up of money paid in entrance-fees, as if religion were a matter of contract. Every man once a month brings some modest coin – or whenever he wishes, and only if he does wish, and if he can; for nobody is compelled; it is a voluntary offering. You might call them the trust funds of piety. (6) For they are not spent upon banquets nor drinking-parties nor thankless eating-houses; but to feed the poor and to bury them, for boys and girls who lack property and parents, and then for slaves grown old and shipwrecked mariners; and any who may be in mines, islands or prisons, provided that it is for the sake of God's school, become the pensioners of their confession.

(7) Such work of love (for so it is) puts a mark upon us, in the eyes of some. "Look," they say, "how they love one another" (for themselves hate one another); "and how they are ready to die for each other" (for themselves will be readier to kill each other). (8) Yes, their indignation at us for using among ourselves the name of "Brothers" must really, I take it, come from nothing but the fact that among them every name of kinship so far as affection goes is false and feigned. But we are your brothers, too, by right of descent from the one mother, Nature – even if you fall short of being men because you are bad brothers. (9) But how much more fittingly are those both called brothers and treated as brothers who have come to know one Father God, who have drunk of one Spirit of holiness, who from one womb of common ignorance have come with wonder to the one light of Truth! (10) But perhaps the reason for our being thought not quite legitimate brothers may be that no tragedy cries aloud of our brotherhood, or because our brotherhood is upheld by the family substance, which among you as a rule dissolves the fraternal tie.

(11) So we, who are united in mind and soul, have no hesitation about sharing property. All is common among us – except our wives ...

(16) Our dinner shows its idea in its name; it is called by the Greek name for love (agape). Whatever the cost, it is gain to spend in piety's name, for with that refreshment we help the needy. No, not, as among you, parasites aspire for the glory of selling their freedom, authorized by their belly to fatten themselves at the cost of any insult; no, because with God there is greater consideration for those of lower degree. (17) If the motive of the banquet is honest, take the motive as the standard of the other proceedings required by our rule of life. Since it turns on the duty of religion, it allows nothing vile, nothing immodest. We do not take our places at table until we have first tasted prayer to God. (18) Only so much is eaten as satisfies hunger; only so much drunk as meets the need of the modest. They satisfy

themselves only so far as men will who recall that even during the night they must worship God; they talk as those would who know the Lord listens. After water for the hands come the lights; and then each, from what he knows of the Holy Scriptures, or from his own heart, is called before the rest to sing to God; so that is a test of how much he has drunk. Prayer in like manner ends the banquet. (19) Then we break up; but not to form groups for violence nor gangs for disorder, nor outbursts of lust; but to pursue the same care for self-control and chastity, as men who have dined not so much on dinner as on discipline.

(20) This gathering of Christians may properly be called illegal, if it is like illegal gatherings; may properly be condemned, if any complain of it on the score on which complaint is made of factious clubs. (21) To whose hurt have we ever met? We are when assembled just what we are when apart; taken together the same as singly; we injure none; we grieve none. When decent people, when good men, gather, when the pious and when the chaste assemble, that is not to be called a faction; it is a Senate. (tr. T. R. Glover, Loeb, 1931)

Tertullian's argument is based on the supposed spirit of the law of associations, which forbids the formation of factions *(factiones)* because these might trouble the public peace. As a consequence, *curia*, a Senate-like meeting on behalf of the public good, would be the correct description of the Christian assembly. The many synonyms used in the text – and this is what astonishes in reading it – demonstrates the lack of a clearly defined legal terminology. The same situation is reflected in the frequently cited passage from Marcianus' third book of *Institutes* (*Dig.* 47.22.1.1):

> Sed religionis causa coire non prohibentur, dum tamen per hoc non fiat contra senatus consultum, quo illicita collegia arcentur.

> But it is not forbidden to come together for purposes of religious practice, so long as there is no breach of the Senate resolution forbidding illegal colleges. (tr. D. Richardson/J. Rüpke)

It is not a question here of a particular privilege for religious associations.[13] This short clause 22 on colleges (in Book 47 of the *Digests*, devoted to criminal law) concerns rather the grey zone in which occasional or regular meetings amount to the illegal formation of associations. Religion is a legitimate cause for assembly (to essay a suitable translation of *coetus*), but even religion may not be instrumental in the formation of

---

[13] For the discussion see again Bendlin 2005, 80–2; my interpretation is even more restrictive.

associations: only in this way, moreover, can sense be made of the rule restricting memberships in colleges to one only (47.22.1.2).

Descriptions of heretics remain accordingly vague, even in the *Codex Theodosianus* (16.5.4):

> Olim pro religione catholicae sanctitatis, ut coetus haeretici usurpatio conquiesceret, iussimus, siue in oppidis siue in agris extra ecclesias, quas nostra pax obtinet, conuentus agerentur, publicari loca omnia, in quibus falso religionis obtentu altaria locarentur.

> We formerly determined, for the good of the religious obligation of 'all-embracing' holiness, and so that the practice of heretical assembly should cease, that, no matter whether assemblies outside the limits of churches that are recipients of our peace take place in cities or in the countryside, all those locations at which altars are set up under the false guise of religious obligation are confiscated. (tr. D. Richardson/J. Rüpke)

Alongside such references to locations and occasional meetings, we find the term "sects", which itself implies supra-regional contexts. The names of such sects typically refer to the deity they "follow"; Tertullian reflects this in the chapter following the one already cited, with his use of the title *Christiani* (*Apol.* 40). *Pagani* thus remained a residual category, describing, as we shall see, individual deviance, neither a sect nor its meetings.

The sources

The most important source for religious law in Late Antiquity is the *Codex Theodosianus*, of which I have already made frequent mention. Promulgated in 438, a century before the *Corpus iuris ciuilis* of the Byzantium-based Emperor Justinian, it represents the first official Roman digest of laws since the Twelve Tables. In its sixteenth book, the *Codex* assembles statutes since the year of Christian toleration in 313, none earlier. Both in its ordering principle and in its editorial treatment of texts, it therefore also bears witness to a fifth-century religious law marked by Christianity; even though, in what follows, I will concentrate predominantly on laws of the fourth century, extensively relying on Roland Delmaire's 2005 commentary.[14]

Older laws are to be found in the still later collection of *Digests* or jurists' commentaries made under Justinian, and in private collections of norms, handed down in fragmentary form or indirectly, such as the *Codex*

[14] Delmaire 2005.

Gregorianus and the *Codex Hermogenianus* from the period of the Tetrarchy.[15] These fragments provide scant material in respect of religion; at the very least, it can be said that they provide no justification for any idea that these collections constituted digests of religion-related laws comparable to the closing book of the *Codex Theodosianus*, or the opening statutes of the *Codex Iustinianus*. Individual fragments, however, show how careful we must be in assuming that religious legislation did not begin until the Christian era. Thus, the *Collatio Mosaicarum et Romanarum legum* from the (presumed) fourteenth book of the *Codex Gregorianus* quotes from a title *De maleficis et Manichaeis* a letter of the tetrarchs that is sated in religious language:

> Sed dii immortales prouidentia sua ordinare et disponere dignati sunt, quae bona et uera sunt, ut multorum et bonorum et egregiorum uirorum ore et sapientissimorum consilio et tractatu inlibata probarentur et statuerentur: quibus nec obuiam ire nec resistere fas est, neque reprehendi a noua uetus religio debet ... hi enim nouellas et inauditas sectas ueterioribus religionibus opponunt, ut pro arbitrio suo prauo excludant, quae diuinitus concessa sunt quondam nobis ... Manichaeos audiuimus nuperrime ueluti noua et inopinata prodigia in hunc mundum de Persica aduersaria nobis gente progressa uel orta esse et multa facinora ibi committere ... (*Coll.* 15.3.2–4)

> But the immortal gods, by their providence, deemed it worthy to ordain and arrange that the things which are good and true would be approved and established in an undiminished state by the counsel and handling of many good and outstanding and very wise men, things which it is evil to obstruct or to resist, and that the old religion should not be refuted by a new religion ... for these are men who set new and unheard sects against the older religions, so that they exclude (the authority) which was once divinely granted to Us ... the Manichees; We have heard that they, as a new and unexpected monstrosity, have recently arisen and progressed into this world from Persia (an enemy nation to Us) and have committed there many crimes ... (tr. Robert M. Frakes, Oxford University Press, 2011, with a correction)

The text displays aversion to religious change, but above all shows the extent to which religion is enlisted as a basis for social values, and for world view in general. In any event, the text takes on a more concrete tone when it comes down to drawing ethnic distinctions. The new religion is classified and denounced as foreign, and in the context of external politics unambiguously hostile.

---

[15] Briefly, Delmaire 2005, 13; more comprehensively on the *Codex Hermogenianus*, Connolly 2010.

If we go still further back, then, apart from the occasional statutory rule encountered on the way, we arrive at the norms in respect of religion contained in the municipal statutes of the early Imperial age. However, as I have demonstrated elsewhere in examining the founding statute of the Roman colony at Urso in Spain,[16] these "constitutions" did not comprise religious laws; they concentrated on the *sacra publica*, the public cult financed or co-financed by the political community (*ciuitas*) in question. They described, in particular, the infrastructure of this segment of religious practice: the priests (*sacerdotes*), who, for their part, were closely aligned with the magistrates. The prerogative of defining the content and definition of the cults initially belonged to the colony's founder, but it did not extend far. This unwillingness to transplant cults is understandable in the context of a "theology of presence", a local conception of the gods.[17]

These laws clearly start from the assumption that there is a broad area of religion that should not be regulated, provided only that it does not interfere with the political and legal structure of the community. This is not a mere isolated circumstance. The centuries-old tradition of founding colonies may have led to a legislative form for such foundations that lagged only a little behind Roman metropolitan legislative techniques, and even offered further-reaching organizational opportunities: in any event, there was never any shortage of new foundations. An inscription from 169 BCE (*AE* 1996, 685), referring to the colony of Aquileia in north-east Italy, already indicates a "constituent" act:

> T(itus) Annius T(iti) f(ilius) tri(um) vir.
> Is hance aedem
> faciundam dedit
> dedicavitque, legesq(ue)
> composuit deditque,
> senatum ter coptavit.

> Titus Annius (Luscus), son of Titus, triumvir. He instigated the construction of this temple and dedicated it. He formulated laws and enacted them. He recruited the Senate three times.

Against this background, the form taken by the rules relating to religion in the Flavian copy of the Julian, thus late Republican, colonial statute of Urso in Hispania Baetica, is significant. The statute did not represent a

[16] Rüpke 2006c, 2006d, 2014a.
[17] See Ando 2008, esp. 144.

legal framework for religion or religions, but a positive definition of central elements of the public cult.

Themes

What themes were addressed by religious legislation in Late Antiquity? What areas were subject to regulation? I should like to investigate three categories of law more closely.

The clergy

Probably the greatest volume of rules was devoted to the priestly domain. This followed a long tradition. Legal norms concerning priests can be traced back to the early Republic. It was rarely a case of defining priesthoods anew, as on the occasion of the foundation of colonies. More often, it was a question of admission criteria and appointment procedures. The perennial problem confronting such legislation was that of regulating a religious institution, willed in the final analysis by the gods, without offending against specifically religious necessities. The method developed in the third century BCE for electing the *pontifex maximus*, by the popular vote of only seventeen of thirty-five *tribus*, in other words by a bare minority of the people, demonstrates the subtlety required in walking such a tightrope; the appointment had previously been made by lot.[18]

Priests constituted the crucial interface between the organized cult and the public administration. John Scheid has fully investigated the alignment of priestly roles with city magistrates, and the limits of that alignment.[19] In terms of the law, it was manifested most of all in the granting of privileges, in fiscal advantages, and in relief from particular public burdens and obligations of service. Owing to their fiscal and legal implications, defining the extent and duration of such privileges required the utmost precision. A rule from the Imperial age, contained in the *Fragmenta Vaticana*, regulates the relief from the *tutela* "of the one who, in the harbour, performs the cult for the welfare of the emperor on the basis of the Archigallus' prophecy" (fr. 148 Huschke). A long series of laws similarly brought the religious specialists of the Christians into the same structure of public roles. Thus the two oldest laws in Book 16 of the *Codex Theodosianus* (16.2.1–2), probably dating from 21 October 313, regulate

---

[18] Cic. *Leg. agr.* 2.16–18, cf. Rüpke 2005a, 15.
[19] Scheid 1985/2001.

exemption from obligations of service. The terminology of the formulae used in the second of these laws reveals the underlying motivation:

> Qui diuino cultui ministeria religionis impendunt, id est hi, qui clerici appellantur, ab omnibus omnino muneribus excusentur, ne sacrilego liuore quorundam a diuinis obsequiis auocentur. (16.2.2)

> Those who perform religious services for the divine cult, that is to say those we call clerics, are to be fully exempt from all other obligations of service, so that nobody motivated by an envy that robs God of his due should distract them from their divine obligations. (tr. D. Richardson/J. Rüpke)

Section 2 on bishops and clerics is one of the longest in Book 16. The chronological sequence in which the rules are set out demonstrates the dual requirement for regulation: while reliefs are given initial prominence, the theme then increasingly turns to the prevention of abuse of the priesthood as a haven from taxation. But this form of deviance can hardly be said to be specifically religious in its motivation!

Here, much more clearly than in the case of the law in respect of associations, and in a sense that is in a way more comparable to the fields of family and inheritance law, indeed private law in general, we perceive the will to translate the internal rules of a particular sphere, that of religion, into the public sphere, the system of rules that apply to everyone. At the beginning of the *Digest* there is a quotation from the Severan jurist Ulpian, defining public law from the perspective of the Republican tradition: *publicum ius in sacris, in sacerdotibus, in magistratibus consistit* – "public law consists of rules of the cult, of priests, and of magistrates" (1.1.1.2). This quotation is preceded by a differentiation between public and private law on the basis of the interests of the common weal and those of the individual in respect of regulation; it is followed by a clarification of the threefold division of private law, in terms of its derivation from natural law, customary law, and civil law. So spheres of regulation as well as sources of law are concerned here. There are no such clarifications in respect of *ius publicum*; here, the remarkable sequence of categories involved in Ulpian's threefold division – itself a familiar form of descriptive definition,[20] but hardly exhaustive in this case – demonstrates the difficulties involved in locating religion in relation to political administration, the interests of the gods in relation to the common weal, within one and the same legal

---

[20] Rüpke 1992.

structure. It also shows a clear desire to draw a veil over the polemic this difficulty gives rise to.

Sacred property

The semantics of the concept of "sacrilege", which appeared (in the Latin) in my earlier quotation, are interesting, as they lead to a second category of norms: property relationships in the religious sphere. The etymology of the words *sacrilegus* and *sacrilegium* is entirely transparent: "taking (away) what is holy" described the theft of the sacral.[21] The term in this technical sense can be found throughout the entire legal tradition. Beyond the bounds of juridical texts, it takes on a further sense, becoming a term of abuse used to describe the extreme of morally unacceptable behaviour. This sense of the word is already attested in Plautus, thus since the earliest literary texts.[22] In the legal tradition, this metaphorical usage is first attested in the religiously charged semantics of Tetrarchic laws;[23] it is then increasingly extended after the 370s, as Delmaire has observed.[24] In 386 a simple breach of Sunday observance suffices to provoke the term.[25]

The persistence of the theme, which also occupies a prominent place in the brief list in Cicero's *Laws* (2.22), is remarkable. It is most acutely and durably delimited in the area of property law (*Dig.* 47.12). Here, punishment for breaches of the norms is declared not to be the affair of the gods: sacrilege is subject to sanctions under criminal law. But the divine property thus protected is precisely demarcated. It comprises property of the gods forming part of the public realm, that is to say sacral spaces that have been established by public dedication (*consecratio*), and the objects they contain. Only they qualify as *sacer* in the technical sense. I must concur with John Scheid's view that, here again, we see clearly the degree of reference made to the responsibility of the community in this area of "public religion".[26] No less interesting, however, is that, in a realm metaphorically far beyond public discourse, sacrilege became a characteristic assigned on an individual basis. It is the original form of religious deviance.

---

[21] Thus Paulus in *Dig.* 48.13.11.
[22] Plaut. *Rud.* 706; *Ps.* 363; see Ter. *Ad.* 304.
[23] See e.g. *Collat.* 6.4 from *Codex Gregorianus* 5: *De nuptiis*.
[24] Delmaire 2005, 66.
[25] Delmaire 2005; *Cod. Theod.* 2.8.18.
[26] Scheid 1981.

Questions arise from this concentration on the public sphere. How was non-public religion treated? The law in respect of graves provides an important answer. From the earliest legal texts onward, it is addressed more widely and with comparable continuity. A grave established by individual resolve and in compliance with the law of property acquired a religious character as soon as it became the resting place of a body or mortal remains. Terminologically, it was then distinguished by the term *religiosus*. Against the background of a continual discourse against lavish graves, these laws were not directed primarily against the theft of movable property (grave robbery), but against alterations to the property "on the ground", in other words change of purpose by commercial use or – above all – further use by an unrelated individual as a place of burial. For all the talk of collective *Di Manes*, the grave was assigned to an individual deceased.

The analogy with sacrilege is clear, as is the clear gradation in the severity of sanction in comparison with offences against divine property qualified as *sacer*. Assimilation to the field of the religious was assured through the agency of priests, more precisely the pontiffs. In Cicero's systematization and in a very few grave inscriptions, they were even assigned legal supervision over both spheres.[27]

Reference to graves does not fully answer the questions arising from the definition of sacrilege. This was also clear to jurists, who, in discussing the law relating to graves, addressed the further area of privately constituted cult structures. But enhancement of status by the presence of the dead body did not apply here. *Sacraria*, cult structures erected on private land or in the home, did not enjoy protection of their legal status as *religiosus*; they could be "freed" of that status.[28] The same *sacra* whose continuity was the subject of juridical discourse were thus in principle conceived of as mobile; their status depended on their longevity in family tradition, not on their presence in the same location. The intrinsic quality of mobility did not, however, distinguish private from public cults. The latter too were in principle regarded as mobile; their complete translocation was as conceivable in Virgil's tales of the flight from Troy as in Camillus' contemporary thought experiment in respect of the proposed removal to Veii after the Gaulish assault, as related by Livy (Livy 5.50–4).[29] The approval

---

[27] Cic. *Leg.* 2.55; *ILS* 1782, 4032; Plin. *Ep.* 10.68–9.
[28] Ulp. *Dig.* 1.8.9.2; cf. Ando 2008, 112–13. This also reflects Aelius Gallus' much older conception in Fest. 424 L.
[29] See Cancik 1995, 2006; Barchiesi 2006; Ando 2008, 110–12.

of the gods affected was invoked in the ritual of *evocatio*; Terminus, the god of boundary stones who when called upon refused his approval, is the exception introduced for the sake of the narrative.[30] But there is no doubt that boundary stones were also mobile following a legal change of ownership; here, too, it is the law relating to land ownership that sanctions religious deviance in the shape of the digging up of boundary stones.[31] Graves too were effectively mobile; in the absence of a monument, memory of the site would scarcely survive a generation's span of some twenty years.

The apparently so clear separation between *sacer* and *religiosus* is further undermined by the narrow definition of *ager publicus*, "public" land, as the basis for consecrations: as this quality of land did not exist in the provinces,[32] generally speaking the distinction existed only in analogy there.[33]

The absence or presence of legal sanctions was not without consequences. Where sanctions existed, they required that boundaries be clearly marked, in a way that went far beyond the architectural marking of a focal centre, whether a temple building or a funerary inscription. While the sacral character of a private location was primarily visible by virtue of its religious use in sacral practices, boundary marks defined a public space as sacred even when it was not being used as such.[34] This was still the nub of the legal problem in the fourth century: private cult locations were identified, not on the basis of architectural features, but by the presence of cult traces (see *Cod. Theod.* 16.10.12). Conversely, as already stated, locations and practices might be separated: Constantine permitted the new construction of a temple of the Gens Flavia (from which his family was descended) at Hispellum, so long as it did not lead to illegitimate practices, or *superstitio* (*CIL* 10.5265). Indeed, temples remained locations of artistic interest and general recreation even after the Theodosian transformation.[35] It is accordingly to practices that we must now turn.

Ritual practices

The norms of the *Codex Theodosianus* are rarely general statutes. The extent of the validity of letters, rescripts, and edicts remains unclear, and this difficulty marks modern academic discussion in respect of constraints on

[30] Livy 1.55.4; Dion. Hal. 3.69.3-6; see Rüpke 1990, 33-4; Ando 2008, 114.
[31] *Dig.* 47.21 for the sanctions.
[32] Plin. *Ep.* 10.48-9.
[33] Gai. *Inst.* 2.5-7; Ulp. *Dig.* 1.8.9, pr. 1.
[34] See Fest. 476.26-9 L on the marking of augural locations by metal stars.
[35] See *Cod. Theod.* 16.10.3; Sauer 2003.

sacrifice between Constantine and the Theodosian codex. Were the same norms repeated owing to non-observance? Were they gradually extended in respect of the practices forbidden? Was their geographical range progressively extended? Despite all differences of opinion, one area of consensus exists, and must be stressed: a central motive for the banning of sacrifices was the intention by so doing to prohibit an important range of divinatory practices.[36]

Divination was understood at the time in question to give access to information regarding future events, including the deaths of emperors and Caesars. This was an old fear, already evident in the early Imperial age. Against the background of a rapid turnover of rulers, not to mention dynasties, the theme had been critical since the third century. A further factor is that the oldest norm against divination in the *Codex Theodosianus* makes a strict distinction between the practice within households and the consultation of auspices in public, thus visibly, even though this might be for private purposes (16.10.1, pr.):

> Imp. Constantinus A(ugustus) ad Maximum. Si quid de palatio nostro aut ceteris operibus publicis degustatum fulgure esse constiterit, retento more ueteris obseruantiae quid portendat, ab haruspicibus requiratur et diligentissime scribtura collecta ad nostra scientiam referatur, ceteris etiam usurpandae huius consuetudinis licentia tribuenda, dummodo sacrificiis domesticis abstineant, quae specialiter prohibita sunt.

> Imperator Constantinus Augustus to Maximus. If part of our palace or of other public buildings is shown to have been struck by lightning, let the *haruspices* investigate the meaning of that in the traditional form, and let a written report be brought to our attention with all prudence. May others also be permitted to use this procedure, so long as they refrain from performing household sacrifices, which are expressly forbidden. (tr. D. Richardson/J. Rüpke)

This instruction to the city prefect, delivered at the end of 320 or the beginning of 321, takes up a prohibition of household haruspices dating from 319 (*Cod. Theod.* 9.16.9).[37] Marie-Theres Fögen has shown that this was not merely a disciplinary question, as the conception of an imperial monopoly of such knowledge had been developing from the start of the Principate and, according to Fögen, in particular since the Severan age. Transcendent knowledge resources and divine revelation were in principle

---

[36] Briefly, Gladigow 2008, 269–71, 276.
[37] Delmaire 2005, 427–8.

and primarily the province of the emperor.[38] The concentration on divination is understandable against this background, as those were the very resources to which divination was designed to provide access.[39]

The desire to control divination had an ancient pedigree, as is shown by the text already cited from the *Collatio legum Mosaicarum et Romanarum* (15.3.2–4). It is, however, important in the context of this inquiry into religious deviance to realize that divination was not regarded merely as a "custom" (*consuetudo*). Increasingly, it was explicitly seen as a religious practice, as something that was closely associated with the usual forms of communication with gods. This too was not new, Cicero himself having assigned the most important divinatory practices to functionaries he classified as *sacerdotes publici* (*Leg.* 2.20–1). In the circumstances of prohibition, however, those same associations had quite different consequences, and the mere frequentation of temples – and so probably having dealings with images of the gods – was liable to the suspicion of serving divinatory practices. It was forbidden (*Cod. Theod.* 16.10.4):

> Placuit omnibus locis adque urbibus uniuersis claudi protinus templa et accessu uetito omnibus licentiam delinquendi perditis abnegari. Volumus etiam cunctos sacrificiis abstinere.

> It has pleased us to decree that temples be immediately closed in all towns and cities, so that, by being forbidden access, all degenerates be deprived of the opportunity to offend. We also desire that everyone refrain from performing sacrifices.

This prohibition, probably dating from 356 CE, was joined by the further ban, to recipients unknown, delivered in the same year (16.10.6):

> Poena capitis subiugari praecipimus eos, quos operam sacrificiis dare uel colere simulacra constiterit.

> We ordain that anyone proved to have engaged in sacrifices or worshipped images be punished by death. (tr. D. Richardson/J. Rüpke)

My assumption that divination was the unspoken target of these norms finds confirmation in the terms of a text addressed to the praetorian prefect Florus in 381, immediately following in the codex (16.10.7):

> Si qui uetitis sacrificiis diurnis nocturnisque uelut uesanus ac sacrilegus, incertorum consultorem se inmerserit fanumque sibi aut templum ad

[38] Fögen 1993.
[39] On the comparability of divination and revelation see Belayche and Rüpke 2007.

hiuscemodi sceleris executionem adsumendum crediderit uel putauerit
adeundum, proscribtione se nouerit subiugandum, cum nos iusta institu-
tione moneamus castis deum precibus excolendum, non diris carminibus
profanandum.

If anyone, be he a madman or someone with contempt for God, in order
to learn what is uncertain is involved in forbidden sacrifices by day or by
night, and believes himself obliged to use a sanctuary or temple to carry
out his crime, or thinks of entering such a place, let him know that he
incurs proscription. Finally, we remind and legally order you that God
be worshipped with pure prayers, not profaned with dreadful hymns. (tr.
D. Richardson/J. Rüpke)

A case reported by Ammianus Marcellinus confirms the drift of these
norms: the defendant, accused of carrying out a sacrifice, is acquitted
because he successfully pleads that he did not perform the sacrifice for
purposes of divination (Amm. Marc. 19.2.12). He clearly did not choose
the defensive strategy of denying having carried out the sacrifice. My
interpretation is further confirmed by the factor that laws of this very
period between the 360s and the 380s, thus delivered in circumstances of
increasingly far-reaching prohibition, display a concern to differentiate. In
the criminal law norms of Book 9, the form of haruspicy that harms no
one is allowed.[40]

While divination and religion were not coterminous categories, from
certain varying perspectives they intersected to a substantial degree. It is
precisely here that prohibitions begin. From here onwards, we find strategic arguments for further prohibitions. Domestic religious practice, not
in principle subject to the monitoring public gaze, becomes the object of
general suspicion. This can be seen most clearly in the hardening of the
prohibition of 381 concerning sacrifices, temple visits, and the worship of
cult images (16.10.10). The substantially more comprehensive version of
392 (16.10.12) seeks to forbid all forms of private urban and rural cult, in
the home or on private land. What seems, however, to be an explicit tar-
geting of *pagani* is merely a variant of a suspicion of the household cult in
general. Kim Bowes has convincingly shown how, in the Christian sphere
too, many distinctions that, superficially, appear dogma-related were in
fact predicated on just such a general suspicion of cult practices in small
circles.[41]

---

[40] *Cod. Theod.* 9.16.7; Delmaire 2005, 86.
[41] Bowes 2007.

We must, nevertheless, not lose sight of the concentration on particular cult practices, the most central of these being animal sacrifice; the additional attempt, cited above, to distinguish between different types of prayer remains an isolated instance. A broad category of practices – for example the use of amulets – is not discussed in the legal texts; votive religion, which formed such an important component of traditional religious practice,[42] is even made an exception, and protected (16.10.8).

> IDEM AAA. PALLADIO DUCI OSDROENAE. Aedem olim frequentiae dedicatam coetui et iam populo quoque communem, in que simulacra feruntur posita artis pretio quam diuinitate metienda iugiter patere publici consilii auctoritate decernimus neque huic rei obreptiuum officere sinimus oraculum. Vt conuentu urbis et frequenti coetu uideatur, experientia tua omni uotorum celebritate seruata auctoritate nostri ita patere templum permittat oraculi, ne illic prohibitorum usus sacrificio rum huius occasione aditus permissus esse credatur.

> The same Augustuses to Palladius, *dux* of Osrhoene.
> By the authority of the public council We decree that the temple shall continually be open that was formerly dedicated to the assemblage of throngs of people and now also is for the common use of the people, and in which images are reported to have been placed which must be measured by the value of their art rather than by their divinity; We do not permit any divine imperial response that was surreptitiously obtained to prejudice this situation. In order that this temple may be seen by the assemblages of the city and by frequent crowds, Your Experience shall preserve all celebrations of festivities, and, by the authority of Our divine imperial response, you shall permit the temple to be open, but in such a way that the performance of sacrifices forbidden therein may not be supposed to be permitted under the pretext of such access to the temple. (tr. Clyde Pharr, 1952)

The concentration on sacrifice may have been due to a variety of motives. We may rather have overestimated the weight of philosophical criticism of sacrifice as a practice not appropriate to a refined conception of deity.[43] It is, however, impossible to overstate here the central role that the practice of sacrifice may have acquired by its emblematic use in the context of the central religious role of the emperor.[44]

---

[42] Van Straten 1981; Beer 1987; Fridh-Haneson 1987; Bouma 1996; Schörner 2003; Todisco 2005; Rüpke 2007b, 154–67; Toorn 2008.
[43] See the critique by Ullucci 2012; cf. Stroumsa 2009; Belayche 2011; Kearns 2011; Pirenne-Delforge and Prescendi 2011; Faraone and Naiden 2012; Münz-Manor 2013.
[44] See for instance Gordon 1990.

Knowledge

Fourth-century laws make no intensive effort to define "paganism" as a *secta*, a religion in its own right. Neither, however, does the *Codex Theodosianus* aim to produce a complete record of illegitimate practices. The focus of its prohibitions is very narrow. Texts betray an awareness of the problem of proof, the problem of evidence, and problems posed by the ambiguities of many practices. What today we routinely call "religion", but in contemporary texts is only occasionally referred to by that name, comes into view above all in the context of divination. Religious deviance is thus religious practice for illegitimate purposes. In contrast with *maleficium*, where sanctions are predicated upon manifest harm, divination is combated on the basis of possible harmful consequences, and the question of legitimate possession of knowledge.

But "knowledge" in the sense used in Book 16 is more than knowledge of divination. The concept of knowledge, which we have already encountered in isolated instances in the late first century BCE and early first century CE, characterizes the entire collection. The first section covers the *fides catholica* (16.1). This is understood as the norm for all peoples, inherited by the Romans from Peter himself (16.1.2). It is defined on the model of sects: it refers to the *Christianorum catholicorum nomen*, which itself constituted the succession of local school leaders. Mentioned by name are the first leader, Peter, and the latest, contemporary leader Damasus (with a reference to Peter, bishop of Alexandria). There is no further explicit definition, although other individuals and groups are referred to as heretics, "sectarians" whose congregations (*conciliabula*) do not merit the name "church" (*ecclesia*; 16.1.2.1). *Sectae* are no longer legitimate variants of a single endeavour. This norm of 380 is preceded by just one (16.1.1) illustrating the practical implications on the basis of a striking example: such people, *homines christianae religionis*, cannot possibly be expected to serve as temple watchmen (364 CE). Anyone who nevertheless expects them to do so will be punished. Individuals' religious knowledge has public consequences that affect everyone.

It is also religious knowledge that is the subject of the final, short title *De religione* of the *Codex*. The final statute of 410 confirms the privileges of the catholic creed, in the face of new, mistaken belief as much as anything else (16.11.3). The preceding edict of 405 to the proconsul of Africa calls for the general dissemination of religious knowledge:

> … uolumus, ut omnibus innotescat dei omnipotentis unam et ueram fidem catholicam, quam recta credulitas confitetur, esse retinendam.

… we desire that it should be made known ever more clearly to everyone that the one and true "catholic" belief in almighty God, confessed in justified credulity, is to be adhered to.

Credulitas no longer indicates *superstitio*. On the contrary, where a particular, unchallenged knowledge is an obligation, "credulity" has become a virtue.

Conclusion

The final section of the *Codex* shows an important step in the development of the concept of religion and the social location of religious deviance. The first law, of 20 August 399, in treating the question of jurisdiction, identifies "religion" as a distinct area within society. This law gives public status to internal religious law and defines its scope, to this extent representing a German-style *Religionsverfassungsrecht*, and under monopoly conditions (16.11.1):

> Quoties de religione agitur, episcopos conuenit agitare; ceteras uero causas, quae ad ordinarios cognitores uel ad usum publici iuris pertinent, legibus oportet audiri.

> Whenever a legal dispute concerning religious practice is entered into, it must be referred to the bishops; other cases, however, which concern regular judges or the realm of public law, must be treated according to the law. (tr. D. Richardson/J. Rüpke)

Parts of the same statute surviving elsewhere in the *Codex* demonstrate that the reference intended here was to religion in general (16.10.17 and 18):

> Vt profanos ritus iam salubri lege submouimus, ita festos conuentus ciuium et communem omnium laetitiam non patimur submoueri. Vnde absque ullo sacrificio atque ulla superstitione damnabili exhiberi populo uoluptates secundum ueterem consuetudinem, iniri etiam festa conuiuia, si quando exigent publica uota, decernimus.
>
> Aedes ilicitis rebus uacuas nostrarum beneficio sanctionum ne quis conetur euertere. Decernimus enim, ut aedificiorum quidem sit integer status, si quis uero in sacrificio fuerit deprehensus, in eum legibus uindicetur, depositis sub officio idolis disceptatione habita, quibus etiam nunc patuerit cultum uanae superstitionis inpendi.

> As we have, in a salutary law, abolished profane rites, we will not allow the abolition of festive assemblies of the citizenry and festive enjoyment shared by all. We accordingly resolve that – barring all sacrifice and damnable

superstition – the people shall be offered enjoyments in accordance with ancient custom, and that festive banquets shall also be held if these serve only the fulfilment of a public vow.

No one is to attempt, on the basis of sanctions we have ordained, to destroy temples that are free of forbidden things. We therefore resolve that the fabric of these buildings is to be maintained intact; if, however, anyone is apprehended in the act of performing sacrifices, legal proceedings are to be initiated against him. After due inquiry, those idols that, even now, might still be the object of worship by vain superstition are to be placed under official supervision. (tr. D. Richardson/J. Rüpke)

A clearly defined terminology is absent, but the concern for semantic demarcation is clear: *profanus ritus, vana superstitio* refer in the abstract to what is forbidden, *uetus consuetudo* to what is allowed. *Dies festus* and *aedes* may continue so long as illegitimate practices, as particularly instanced by *sacrificia*, are absent. Even images of deities are worthy of preservation as works of art – the term, if not used here, is certainly to be found elsewhere – if religious activity is excluded. The strategy being followed, rather than Christianization, is one of reference to and safeguarding by the emperor. It is narrowly defined by the separation of religion from the public realm. The consequences of internal religious jurisdiction are restricted, circumscribed by the claims of the emperor and by custom and tradition;[45] it would be a long time before appropriate cultural terms would be invoked in respect of the antithesis described here.

The outlines of the religion-related norms of the *Codex Theodosianus* become still clearer when compared with Cicero's religious legislation, both in where they agree and where they differ. The role of priests is central to both projects, although the identity of those priests changes. *Sacerdotes* or clerics symbolically designate the religious realm. They hold it together by virtue of their knowledge and/or their jurisdiction. They constitute a material part of its infrastructure, and enjoy corresponding privileges. On the other hand, in the *Codex* spatial definition of religion has become less important;[46] Cicero's demand for religious locations to have a clear identity has evolved into clear constraints as to which sites are to be regarded as legitimate. Where these are not churches, by the end of the fourth century they have become mere popular or heretical places of assembly; at most, locations for aesthetic distraction. The decline of

---

[45] Cf. Kahlos 2009, 107, who sees here only isolated, ad hoc norms.
[46] Cf. Ando 2008, who arrives at the same observation, but on the basis of different texts.

the main distinction between *sacer* and *profanus*, originally defining the meaning of *sacrilegus*, opened the opportunity to use the latter as a merely pejorative term, even in legal texts.

But the distinction between public and private remains important and problematical. The legitimacy of the private and domestic in the religious realm has become reduced, even if explicit prohibitions remain isolated occurrences. On practical grounds at least, interest and legislation now concentrate principally on the public and visible domain.

The formulation of actual religious norms – which (especially in the texts of the *Codex Theodosianus*) are not themselves elaborated in detail – is left to traditional bodies. These are distinguished by continuity of personal referents and local legitimacy: guarantors of correctness are the *maiores* or Peter; and both, of course, spoke in Rome and to the Romans. Here in any event the later text is more explicit. The Rome of Late Antiquity is the world's norm; for Cicero, the opinions of his Italian forefathers too might have enduring validity, and the universality of his statutes have to be proved by their compatibility with what is held to be correct in Greece. Where Cicero, and the Tetrarchan fragments too, legislated religion from the inside, from the core of the legal establishment, the legislation of Late Antiquity under investigation here increasingly acquired a bird's-eye perspective, defining the place of religions in the community and demarcating them as an "other", an *aliud*. Here in fact were laid the foundations of a specifically European approach to the legal regulation of religion.

The contribution that my analysis brings to the question of religious deviance has remained limited. The prominent role played in the politics of prohibition by divination, and private divination in particular, nevertheless points to a further, new focus of ancient discourse regarding religious deviance. The stumbling block was unmediated and unmonitored access to authentic knowledge of the divine will or the divine world order. Such knowledge was facilitated in particular by sacrifices, the frequentation of temples, and direct access to images of the gods. These three practices became the object of other kinds of criticism too, but that older critique of sacrifices and images, and, as we have seen, temples, played no significant role in the legal texts. Any individual search for authentic religious knowledge, where it did not "credulously" adopt the pre-formulated doctrinal credo, became suspect.

CHAPTER 6

The individual in a world of competing religious norms

Inclusion and exclusion

The definition of deviance cited at the beginning of this book includes the infringement of general societal norms and such social norms as have been formulated by individual groups in society.[1] Our investigation of laws of the late fourth century has revealed that account was taken of the formulation of such norms within religious groups or traditions. The assignment of judicial office to bishops in matters related to religion applied only to Christianity, or, more precisely, to "catholic" Christianity (by no means to be equated with the "Roman Catholic Church" after the schism of the late Middle Ages and the post-Reformation process of "confessionalization"). Other laws in *Codex Theodosianus* 16 show, however, that Judaism was similarly addressed, although without being granted a legal privilege: the patriarchate's freedom of action was first restricted, and the institution then dissolved.[2]

It is possible to trace the development of such internal processes of normalization by means of the texts they produced. The chronology of that development in the case of the Mishnah presents difficulties.[3] In this instance, processes since the second and third centuries had led to a comprehensive formulation of norms enabling a Judaism robbed of its ritual and institutional centre, Jerusalem, to be expressed through the conduct of each individual, especially male, Jew within the small but growing minority represented by rabbinic Judaism.[4] The linguistic forms employed in the Mishnah indicate a clear reference to contemporary Roman law, which also lent the rabbinical authors a corresponding degree of authority.[5] However, Daniel Boyarin has pointed out that the very multiplicity

---

[1] See p. 3.
[2] See e.g. *Cod. Theod.* 16.8.8.
[3] Neusner 1991, Introduction.
[4] Fonrobert 2013.
[5] Lightstone 2002.

of named spokespersons documented signifies the renunciation of an exclusive definition of Jewish life: in conscious contrast to the Christian churches, the rabbis had in fact no desire to turn Judaism into a religion.[6] The parallels with the procedure of the Latin digests are not accidental: here in Justinian's codification is collected precisely the material that, while not contained in the directly applicable norms of the *Codex Iustinianus*, is calculated to be of aid in its interpretation.

The strategy of the great Christian churches was a different one, developed, and still at the time in question in process of development, out of the institutionalization of those elements that distinguished them from Judaism.[7] The canones attributed to a supposedly early fourth century council at the Spanish town of Elvira (Illibera), some of which going back to the latter half of the fourth century, already contained forms of *anathemata*, or rules of exclusion. Here we find an enormous change from the New Testament scriptures, which, yet to be formerly canonized, were still dominated by reformulations of Hellenistic caste-based social codes.

Both the locations where religious deviance was to be found and the content of the associated norms changed. When we have cast our gaze back to the Hellenistic–Republican age, and to Imperial age legislation and philosophical discourse in both its political and its social context, results have been limited. The various normative texts are, on the whole, restrained, and scarcely comparable with the detailed approach of a Theophrastus. Besides the problem of insufficient religious knowledge, which can be traced from Cicero (and especially Varro) to the turn of the fourth century, that of individual religious experience – at special places, before images of the gods, in divination – played a particular role, constituting a particular source of religious deviance. Even in making this observation, however, we tread a precarious path: for individual religious experience was at the same time fundamental to the Romans' view of religion.

Individual religious experience

The same Seneca who, in his treatise *De superstitione*, polemicizes against emotionalization and the unfolding of individual religious experience in

---

[6] Boyarin 2004a and 2006; see also Burrus et al. 2006.

[7] For the recent discussion of the "parting of the ways" as a process still going on in Late Antiquity, see Reed 2003; Goodman 2003; Fredriksen 2003; Boyarin 2003, 2004a; Dohrmann and Reed 2013; for the institutional development see also Barceló 2013.

temples, we find in letter 41 of the *Epistulae morales* taking religion institutionalized in temples as the starting point for a reflection on religious
experience (41.1–3):

> Non sunt ad caelum eleuandae manus nec exorandus aedituus, ut nos
> ad aurem simulacri, quasi magis exaudiri possimus, admittat: prope est a
> te deus, tecum est, intus est. (2) Ita dico, Lucili: sacer intra nos spiritus
> sedet, malorum bonorumque nostrorum obseruator et custos: hic prout a
> nobis tractatus est, ita nos ipse tractat. Bonus uero uir sine deo nemo est
> … (3) Si tibi occurrerit uetustis arboribus et solitam altitudinem egressis
> frequens lucus et conspectum caeli roamorum aliorum alios protegentitum
> <prouentu> summouens, illa proceritas siluae et secretum loci et admir-
> ation umbrae in aperto tam densae atque continuae fidem tibi numinis
> faciet. Si quis specus saxis penitus exesis montem suspenderit, non manu
> factus, sed naturalibus causis in tantam laxitatem excauatus, animum
> tuum quadam religionis suspicione percutiet. Magnorum fluminum cap-
> ita ueneramur; subita ex abdito uasti amnis eruption aras habet; coluntur
> aquarum calentium fonts, et stagna quaedam uel opacitas uel inmensa alti-
> tude sacrauit.

> You are doing an excellent thing, one which will be wholesome for you, if, as
> you write me, you are persisting in your effort to attain sound understanding;
> it is foolish to pray for this when you can acquire it from yourself. We do not
> need to uplift our hands towards heaven, or to beg the keeper of a temple to
> let us approach his idol's ear, as if in this way our prayers were more likely to
> be heard. God is near you, he is with you, he is within you. (2) This is what
> I mean, Lucilius: a holy spirit indwells within us, one who marks our good
> and bad deeds, and is our guardian. As we treat this spirit, so are we treated
> by it. Indeed, no man can be good without the help of God …
>
> (3) If ever you have come upon a grove that is full of ancient trees which
> have grown to an unusual height, shutting out a view of the sky by a veil
> of pleached and intertwining branches, then the loftiness of the forest, the
> seclusion of the spot, and your marvel at the thick unbroken shade in the
> midst of the open spaces, will prove to you the presence of deity. Or if a
> cave, made by the deep crumbling of the rocks, holds up a mountain on its
> arch, a place not built with hands but hollowed out into such spaciousness
> by natural causes, your soul will be deeply moved by a certain intimation
> of the existence of God. We worship the sources of mighty rivers; we erect
> altars at places where great streams burst suddenly from hidden sources; we
> adore springs of hot water as divine, and consecrate certain pools because
> of their dark waters or their immeasurable depth. (tr. E. Philipps Barker,
> OUP, 1932)

I shall not continue the quotation here, even though the stoical doctrine
of the divine character of the soul – and its perpetual communication

with the divine[8] – developed further on in the letter is highly significant
for the history of religious individualization. But my intention here is not
to give the text a modernistic reading, as an accolade to natural religion as
opposed to institutionalized religion forced into the confines of (church)
architecture. The text is much too traditional for that, belonging in a long
tradition of Greek philosophical religious criticism involving a critique of
polytheism and the cult of images.[9]

This text meant as a critique is also involuntarily traditional, and even
affirmative. Seneca's assumption is that religious experience leads to the
institutionalization of cult activity: *ueneramur, aras habet, coluntur, sacrauit*
(41.3). What I call "religious experience" he conceives here as a process in
several stages: a fortuitous (*occurrerit*, 3) aesthetic perception leads to an
emotional reaction (*admiratio*); this he regards as elusive, perhaps even
pre-verbal. But the religious character of the experience comes as if impos-
ing itself from outside; the recipient of the sensation also remains passive
here: *fidem tibi numinis faciet, animum tuum quaedam religionis suspicione
percutiet* (3). Seneca is at pains to represent even the resulting cult not
as a human institution – Varro's constant, nagging didacticism! – but as
something simply given, with no human creative agent. In the sequence
of reactions cited above, the only verb with a human subject is even a
deponent, with passive voice: *ueneramur*.

Seneca consciously locates his examples in a nature unaltered by human
beings, portraying a rural idyll that in fact, however, has more the air of
parkland than of inaccessible "wilderness".[10] It is a city dweller's image of
nature, and as such comparatively new to Rome.[11] So far as the quality and
consequences of religious experience are concerned, the trope is polemical and unnecessary; Seneca indicates at the beginning of the letter that
the religious experiences are made in the centres of urban life, namely
in temples; the attempt to approach close to the image of the god is the
behaviour he rejects; but, as we know from *De superstitione*, this is just the
behaviour that produces intense emotional reactions. Under the conditions of a polytheistic religion, the religious experience described does not
lead to a nameless cult. The source has a name; the altar names the divine
addressee. In an environment of houses and cities, pictorial representation

---

[8] Sen. *Ep.* 41.5: *conuersatur quidem nobiscum, sed haeret origini suae* ... See Setaioli 2007, 350 for the origin of this conception and its development in Seneca; see also Setaioli 2013.

[9] Athanassiadi and Frede 1999; Gladigow 2008; Tanaseanu-Döbler 2009.

[10] This also differs generally from the tradition of (theoretical rather than practical) observation of the cosmos, see Setaioli 2007, 334–5.

[11] See Cancik 1998, 55–62.

suggests itself as a means to take the linguistic identification further, and intensify the "re-presentation".

If Seneca may be represented as a leading advocate of the positive evaluation of religious experience, public practices too may be cited in favour of such a positive evaluation of individual access to divination. In the context of auspices, the reading of omens from the flight of birds, it was an announcement by one individual, the magistrate, in many instances an augur, that led to the interruption of political business. It was in this way that the consul Bibulus, in his conflict with his colleague C. Iulius Caesar in 59 BCE, was able to assume that he could sabotage the latter's legislative intentions by the mere announcement that he, Bibulus, "would observe the heavens" (*de caelo servare*). Such a "private revelation", more precisely the announcement of a communication with Jupiter, was evidently regarded as sufficient for the purpose. This shows the value placed on individual religious experience among the political elite. But it is no wonder that the obligatory aspect of such episodes could quickly become a cause of conflict.[12]

The priority given to individual initiatives

The priority given to individual communication with the gods also applied when the claims of social obligation and individual freedom of action were particularly in conflict. When an army was being raised (*dilectus*), an individual could temporarily avoid conscription on religious grounds. The author Cincius (Gell. *NA* 16.4.4), probably active in the early Augustan age, counts among such exceptional circumstances a family burial and the subsequent period of ritual mourning (*feriae denicales*), an epileptic fit (*morbus sonticus*), and receiving auspices that necessitate ritual expiation (*piaculum*). The particular situation is characterized by the fact that the delay for the ten-day period of mourning applies only if the *feriae* have not been arranged for the express purpose of forestalling an appearance before the recruiting officer.[13]

Up to now, our analysis of laws and discussions by jurists has revealed two further areas where individual initiatives are given public, legal safeguard. The first concerns graves. As *loca religiosa*, these enjoyed particular protection. I have already indicated elsewhere that, while the quality of *sacer* was omitted with a view to preserving a terminological distinction

---

[12] See Rüpke 2011c.
[13] See also Rüpke 1990.

vis-à-vis "public" cults, the purpose of employing the pontiffs was pre-cisely to obtain public protection.[14] If we are to take seriously the formula *Di Manes* (of a particular person), which dominated first-century grave-stones, we have to see in it the institution of a new cult, although one that bound only the particular individual's immediate family. It would, however, have been all the more important to ensure a secure foundation for the public relationship entailed by such a project, in terms of property law and religion. Cicero devotes approximately one half of his commen-tary on religious laws to just this kind of question (Cic. *Leg.* 2.46–68), and is well aware of the particular emphasis this gives to the structure of his text. It is Atticus, his interlocutor, who introduces this section with: *Nunc de sacris perpetuis et de Manium iure restat* (2.45) – "Now we must deal with perpetual cults, and the law concerning the dead." It is indicative of Cicero's perception of the problem that he closes the section with a gener-alizing rule: the choice of burial place for the dead must not disadvantage the living (2.67). Religious action on the part of the individual must be guided by simple, straightforward norms, and can only be based on the internalization of such norms.

But, in the case of *sacra publica* too, it was as a rule individuals who intro-duced new deities, on the basis of their own family- or situation-related intuitions. Adoption of such deities, entailing all the public obligations (including financing) implied by the designation *sacra publica*, depended, of course, on a resolution of the Senate. And yet the introduction of a new cult, the dedication of a new statue, entailed the possibility of formulating and introducing religious norms that were binding on the community; and such norms could be very detailed.[15] Such a normative act would of course build on a shared consensus within the community,[16] but room would remain for individual touches.

The lengthy process of discussing and regulating private cults (*sacra privata*) did not, however, concern the adoption of new cults as much as the continuity of old ones beyond the death of the *pater familias*. The story of the perpetuation of the cult of Hercules using public funding and state slaves (*servi publici*), after the Pinarii and Potitii had been relieved of this task,[17] demonstrates how important it was that a cult should be allowed to continue

---

[14] See Rüpke 1990, ch. 5.3.2.

[15] E.g. *CIL* 8.620 = 11796 = *ILS* 4908 from the temple of Apollo at Mactar on the statue of Diana donated by Sextus Iulius Possessor in the second half of the second century CE.

[16] Vigourt 2011, 84.

[17] Liv. 9.29.9–11; Servius *ad Aen.* 8.179.

in an appropriate form. Appius Claudius Caecus did not wait for the two clans to die out before taking this step at the end of the fourth century BCE.

Potential conflicts

The prioritizing of private religious initiatives conceals a potential for conflict. The concern for cult continuity as against the allure of *hereditas sine sacris* might suggest a process of "secularization", a reduction in the expenditure of material and immaterial resources on religion. Academic research has in fact chosen this very perspective frequently enough, and understood Varro's *Antiquitates* and Augustus' temple restoration projects as pure conservation politics.[18] This approach is false. Cicero makes that clear with the initial *ne* of the first relevant rule of his *constitutio religionum*. His norms are directed against innovations.[19]

The background to Cicero's project is not the Bacchanalia case of 186 BCE; it is worth noting how casually this case is mentioned – as an example of ancient severity (*severitatem maiorum*) – in just one sentence of Cicero's commentary on his own legal text (Cic. *Leg.* 2.37). Even though, in striving for timeless validity, he avoids obvious current references – Cicero prefers to speak of circumstances in Greece – the problem of Egyptian gods must have been a present issue for him. The followers of Isis had entered the purview of the magistrates only a few years before; a temple had been destroyed on the Capitol, in the heart of the city.[20]

Cicero talks of *deos advenas* and *adscitos*, immigrant and imported gods (2.19), and he and his contemporaries may have associated religious innovation by individuals mainly with a mobility that had long passed beyond the confines of the Graeco-Italian world, in which the Dionysus cult in Rome may well have had its origins. The trend had been heralded by the conflicts of the second century BCE: the expulsion of Jews and Chaldeans[21] – whatever the ethnicity of those affected may have been – indicates a supra-regional issue. The Roman policy of involvement in the eastern Mediterranean, with the naturalization of the *Mater deorum magna Idaea*, Cybele from Pessinus, had already itself enlarged the geographical context; Cicero formulates special rules precisely for this cult (*Leg.* 2.22). Rome's attitude towards the eunuch priests of Cybele, the *galli* or *galloi*,

---

[18] Challenged by Galinsky 2007.
[19] Cf. Lafond 2009 on the frequent talk of *nomoi* for bolstering tradition in Hellenistic cities.
[20] Brief summary in Mora 1990.
[21] See Cramer 1954.

demonstrates the desire to embrace the religious gain represented by such a cult importation while isolating the deviant practices associated with it.

This species of horizontal mobility might of course be accompanied by other innovations effected by transfers into the cult from textual media, as instanced by the many personifications that arose in the latter years of the fourth century BCE.[22] Cicero had his eye on this area too, and probably with less thought of the private cult (2.28); although the separation of public and private is here merely political, important only for the public realm, not affecting the religious dimension as such. The structures of "public" and private religion in essence corresponded here, which may have been highly significant in providing a basis for the reception and legitimation of publicly financed religion at the time. These were processes of institutionalization, having a decisive effect on a cult's status, which, in turn, affected the manner of people's dealings with it. John Scheid was able to show this clearly in respect of deviance in the area of public cults: regardless of the individual genesis of a cult, the entire citizenry was affected insofar as it communicated on a social and religious level with the cult, or included members of it.[23]

Problems of conceptualization

While focusing his analysis on the gods, Cicero knew that this approach would not yield an appropriate description of the problem he was seeking to address. In the continuation of his text he turns his attention to rituals, and reformulates his initial rule: *Ex patriis ritibus optuma colunto* – "Of the ancestral rites the best shall be preserved" (2.22).[24] He then establishes a specific rule for the cult of Cybele; here too, however, he offers no conceptual frame for what is not allowed, for what is deviant.

The systematization of cults was already well advanced by the second century CE. The lexicographer Festus offers not only a clear-cut distinction between public and private cults, but a list of subcategories in addition (Festus p. 284, 18–21 L):

> Publica sacra, quae publico sumptu pro populo fiunt, quaeque pro montibus, pagis, curis, sacellis: at privata, quae pro singulis hominibus, familiis, gentibus fiunt.

---

[22] See Clark 2007.
[23] Scheid 1981, 154.
[24] The commentary is astonishingly frank in presenting the circularity of the argument. As traditions change, the oldest and closest to the gods must be regarded as the best (2.40).

The public cults are those that are celebrated at public expense in the interest of the [Roman] people, and those that are in the interest of the hills [the Septimontium], the *pagi* [surrounding villages], the *curiae* [the thirty Romulan "districts"], and the "shrines" [perhaps the twenty-seven shrines of the Argei within the Servian Wall]. Private cults on the other hand are those established in the interest of individuals, families, and *gentes* ["clans" sharing the same *nomen*]. (tr. D. Richardson/J. Rüpke)

This classification may go back to Festus' most important source, the Late Augustan Verrius Flaccus, as the same categories are to be found in the Augustan historian Dionysius of Halicarnassus (*Roman Antiquities* 2.65.2). Macrobius in Late Antiquity, probably basing his account on the same source, relates something about feast days observed by individuals (*feriae … singulorum*), listing birthdays, actions in response to lightning strikes, burials, and expiations (*Saturnalia* 1.16.8).

It is clear that the typology of social forms of religion constructed on the basis of such categories does not coincide with the social groups who celebrated the cults in question. The entire area of the religious activities of priestly colleges is missing. The terminology used reflects a harmonious social ideal, beginning with the household and proceeding via the *gentes* to the public level, both the particular and the general. It tells us nothing about the reality of divergent interests, social barriers, physical mobility, and individual isolation.[25] There is no mention of any category of "elective cults".

Similarly, no attention is given to the implications of mobility. The few concepts Festus supplies – elsewhere of course, and again possibly relying on Verrius[26] – clearly reveal the limitations of his proposed system.

Peregrina sacra appellantur, quae aut euocatis dis in oppugnandis urbibus Romam sunt †conata†, aut quae ob quasdam religiones per pacem sunt petita, ut ex Phrygia Matris Magnae, ex Graecia Cereris, Epidauro Aesculapi. Quae coluntur eorum more, a quibus sunt accepta. (Fest. 268 L)

What we call foreign cults are those celebrated for gods that were summoned to Rome on the occasion of its conquests of other cities, or were imported in peacetime on the grounds of some religious consideration or other, instances being the cult of the Great Mother from Phrygia, of Ceres from Greece, and of Aesculapius from Epidaurus. These are worshipped according to the manner of the peoples from whom they were taken. (tr. D. Richardson/J. Rüpke)

---

[25] Rüpke 2007b, 24.
[26] Also the view of Ando 2008, 134.

The definition shows this to be a summary of the cults described by Cicero as *publice acceptos*, with the addition of the gods cited.[27] These gods too are to be worshipped by means of the traditional rituals. They thus remain phenomenologically "foreign" (but not hostile); no account is taken of the onset of assimilation from the very beginning.

The same rules are in evidence in respect of a further concept of the same type:

> Municipalia sacra uocantur, quae ab initio habuerunt ante ciuitatem Romanam acceptam; quae obseruare eos uoluerunt pontifices, et eo more facere, quo adsuessent antiquitus. (Fest. 146.9–12 L)

> Those cults are called municipal that originally belonged to provincial cities before they assumed Roman citizenship. The pontiffs wished the inhabitants to continue those cults, and to celebrate them as had been their custom since ancient times. (tr. D. Richardson/J. Rüpke)

"Every community has its religion, as we have ours", states Cicero in his speech on behalf of Flaccus (*Flacc.* 69). While this model eases the way to conceiving of the "religion" of other communities, it sheds no light on the emergence or continuance of social groups or networks by means of religion. In any event, the concepts developed to deal with this problem were not "religion" and its plural, but two others from another field.[28]

Secta, evidently a translation of the Greek *hairesis*, was primarily used to differentiate the philosophical schools of the early Hellenistic age, but could also refer to Jewish groups such as the Sadducees and Pharisees (for example in Acts 4:17; Josephus, *Jewish War* 2.8.1). The term is rare in Cicero, who uses it more for political (for example, *Letters to Brutus* 10.1) than for philosophical groups (for example, *Pro Caelio* 40; *Brutus* 120); but it occurs frequently after the first century CE. Tertullian explicitly uses the term in the latter philosophical sense (*Apologeticum* 3.6; 40.7; 46.2), to imply a legitimate choice between comparable options. At the beginning of the fourth century, the term is no longer used by Lactantius and Firmicus as a self-description in apologetic texts, but it does occur in the so-called Edict of Tolerance in 313.[29] Here, Licinius looks back to his earlier attempt to bring Christians "back to their senses", after they had abandoned the "sects of their parents" (34.1). The term is very frequently used in respect of "catholic sects", as well as heretical and all other variations of

---

[27] See Ferri 2010.
[28] See Rüpke 2009d, 340–1.
[29] Lactantius, *On the Deaths of the Persecutors* 34.

sects to be found in the collection of norms contained in Book 16 of the *Codex Theodosianus* (especially 16.5), even though 16.6.50 stresses that all belong to *una perfidia*.[30] It must, however, be emphasized that mentions of "catholic" or "orthodox" sects remained rare. On the other hand, the Latinized loan word *haeresis* became increasingly important for the exclusively negative connotation of illegitimate separatism. This is abundantly clear in Tertullian's text *Objections against the Heretics* (*De praescriptione haereticorum*).[31]

Another term derived from the area of philosophical schools was *disciplina*. It could describe both the intellectual content of a branch of knowledge and a way of life. *Disciplina magorum, Etruscorum, Chaldaica, augurum*, and *rei publicae* are expressions from the first century BCE; already in the second century BCE Cato the Elder warns against "foreign discipline" (1.4). Military discipline remained the underlying idea, directly or metaphorically, but without excluding any other developing contexts. For example, Apuleius makes very frequent use of the word in the second century CE, offering expressions such as *diuinae disciplinae* (magic) and *ex disciplina sectae* (*Metamorphoses* 3.19.4; 4.18), and *incuria uerae disciplinae* as an anthropological characterization (*De deo Socratis* 3). Tertullian at the turn of the same century uses the term for new attributes of the Christian way of life (*Adversus Marcionem* 4.36; *De jejuniis* 12), although it is almost entirely absent from Latin translations of the New Testament (apart from seven instances in Paul). Minucius Felix, writing a little later, provides no further terminological precision, although he emphasizes the idea of a new way of life (for example, 5.1), and applies the term *disciplina* to traditional cults too (6.1; 8.2; 30.3). For Christians, *disciplina* is something that has to be developed (35.3). Finally, Firmicus in the fourth century, in *De errore profanorum religionum* (18.1), is able to polemicize against the "devil's discipline" (*diaboli … disciplina*).

In contrast to usage in respect of the term *religio*, the terminology for religious groups was straightforward. A multitude of comparable elective options could be described as equivalents of philosophical schools. This, importantly, implied a basic core of knowledge in respect of a particular lifestyle. Use of the term *disciplina* enabled the approach to be used when referring to particular types of religious specialists such as magicians, haruspices, and even augurs; and this as early as the late Republic. In Latin

---

[30] On the terminology applying to religious groups in the *Codex* see Zinser 2002.
[31] Pieper, Schimmelpfennig, and von Soosten 2003, 9. I thank Claus-Jürgen Thornton for drawing my attention to this and to the term *Chrestianismos*.

texts, the usage was nevertheless not extended to a wider selection of religions until the Christian apologists adopted it at the end of the second century, and it did not reach official texts before the fourth century.

Terminological developments went in parallel with religious developments, the development of doctrine and group ethics, and the concern to mark limits: with violence in extreme instances, but above all with stories of violence.[32] These were protracted developments, and for the most part came much later than Cicero's terminology, mentioned at the beginning of this section on conceptualizations. Guy Stroumsa, in a series of lectures given at the Collège de France, describes the destruction of the Temple in Jerusalem as the decisive turning point in the development of Judaism and nascent Christianity, and in the history of religion in the Mediterranean world in general; the destruction itself and its confirmation as irrevocable by the suppression of Bar Kochba's rebellion were epoch-making events.[33] Ignatius, intent on making his own lifestyle an issue, was yet to coin, in Antioch, the Greek expression *Chrestianismos*. Cicero had operated in an entirely different context.

[32] The comparative approach of Sizgorich 2009 has been of aid here.
[33] Stroumsa 2008; Vinzent 2014.

CHAPTER 7

Deviance and individuation: from Cicero to Theodosius

Loci and targets of normative processes in the first century BCE

"We" became problematic for Cicero. On the surface, and in rhetorical mode, he promotes universality in the text of *Laws*: universality on a basis of natural law, as he amply expounds in the first and second books of the work;[1] and particularly in respect of religion. The world comprises a unity of gods and humans: *uniuersus hic mundus una ciuitas communis deorum atque hominum existimanda* – "this entire world must be regarded as a polity shared in common between gods and humans" (1.23). Religious practice too can thus be arrived at on the basis of natural law: *omnisque natura coniunctos suos duxerit, cultumque deorum et puram religionem susceperit ...* – "and all nature saw that her members were joined, and took up the cult of the gods and simple piety ..." (1.60). The *leges de religione* (2.17) accordingly apply to "all good and strong peoples, not the Roman people alone" (*non enim populo Romano sed omnibus bonis firmisque populis leges damus*, 2.35). This avowal makes it clear that Cicero is not using the concept he previously expounded, that of two fatherlands (*duas esse ... patrias*), or even dual citizenship (*<duas> habet civitatis*, both expressions from 2.5), to differentiate religious practices. And the *municipalia sacra* too are the affair of the Roman pontiffs, at a supervisory level at least.[2]

And yet, at the same time, Cicero is promoting exclusion. He in fact designates as "good and strong peoples", apart from the Romans, only the Greeks. The rules as formulated must ensure that the legitimate traditions of the Greeks too should count among those permitted, and the commentary repeatedly makes this clear.[3] Here alongside a "we" appears a "you"

---

[1] For a full account see Girardet 1983.
[2] See Chapter 2, section "Cicero".
[3] E.g. 2.26, 28, 29, 35–41, 45, 56, 59, 62–7, 69. The same also applies, of course, to instances of Greek religion in Asia Minor.

(directed at Atticus), which, however, binds the two peoples together. But the extent to which exclusion is in fact being promoted under the pretext of universality becomes all the clearer; and the principle is no longer descriptive, but normative: religious alternatives have – implicitly – become deviant.

We must look again, and more closely. Italy was no longer a problem; more precisely, it was a problem that was regarded as solved, as is shown by the passage concerning two fatherlands and one citizenship.[4] Cicero himself as a young man had experienced the Social War, which lay scarcely more than a generation in the past. Varro, who was ten years older than him, had a sharper perception of such differences within Italy, as is shown by his reference to the Bacchus procession in Lavinium (*Ant. rer. div.* fr. 262 Cardauns). The far-flung world had been conquered, by Pompey and Caesar; defeats such as Carrhae, where Crassus died in 53 BCE, took place on the distant military and geographical frontiers of the Mediterranean world, and did not (yet) signal cultural contacts. Only a few years later in *De natura deorum*, after a round of the Civil War fought in Syria and Alexandria, Cicero would also turn his attention to Egyptian and Indian divinities: but still to dismiss them as harmless exotica.[5] In *Laws* they remained entirely invisible: although Isis – with the aid of Roman worshippers of both sexes – had long since reached the Capitol.

Any normative characterization of a historically contingent situation, that of late Republican "Roman" religion, turns out to be based on a very selective description of what was actually happening. Parts of the "we" comprising the Roman people were, in religious terms, deviant, and had to be brought back to the correct path. Cicero may have seen the successful banishment of the Isis cult from the Capitol as a signal that such a corrective strategy might be successful. The removal of deviance might stabilize society. The prominence given to the injunction that no one may have "separate" gods belies any notion that Cicero was overly optimistic in this regard. Civil war was still simmering in the streets: I am thinking of the confrontation between Milo and Clodius in the year 52. Marcus roundly accuses Clodius in the *De legibus*, under the headings *poena uiolati iuris* (2.22) and *poena uiolatae religionis* (2.41), and is satisfied to note Clodius' death and lack of a burial (2.42). That this concrete instance of a criminal religious deviance is treated under the heading of the most general formulation possible points to the limits of the systematics of Cicero's

[4] Cic. *Leg.* 2.5.
[5] See Cic. *Nat.* 3.39, 42, 54, and Rüpke 2012a.

approach. Thus, as I began by suggesting, Cicero's injunction must be seen as indicating a continuing problem.

Against first appearances, however, the same injunction also indicates a success. Cicero is not writing laws merely from the perspective of institutionalized public control by the priesthoods he describes so comprehensively. His text unfolds against the background of a morality suffused with aristocratic virtues. These are plainly listed in the first book: *liberalitas, patriae caritas, pietas, bene merendi de altero … uoluntas, referendae gratiae uoluntas* – "generosity, love of homeland, the sense of family, the constant will to do good to others and to show gratitude" (1.43). But this *constitutio religionum* is addressed to all citizens, assuming a generalization of the ideal standards of the elite. This becomes clear when we realize that the important priesthoods had not been opened to plebeians until the *lex Ogulnia* of 300 BCE. The question as to whether only patricians might have the established right to observe auspices would continue to be controversial into the Augustan era.

This process of popularization led to an increase in social discipline,[6] as can also be detected in other Hellenistic cities: Theophrastus' portrayal of a *deisidaimon* distinctly precedes Cicero's statutes. Here is where our reflections in the first chapter, on the functionality of deviance, bear fruit. It is precisely under the conditions of a generalized, democratized "we" that the constant reminder of the other, of an image that is harmless for all its strangeness, and, when all is said and done, part of the same society, acquires its function. The foolishness on the public square, as described by Seneca and Plutarch in Chapter 4, make of that image of the other a stereotype, confronting us with the face of deviance. The evidence that these instances of foolishness are in fact performed by a fool, who behaves no differently in his own home, is important: deviance is shown to be "sick", having the aspect of a psychological tic. This suggests that the public square had become a stage where personalities, individuals, performed; a place where they displayed themselves as they were. And, because it was now necessary to show that one was as one had to be in order to be acceptable in public, that public norm, by transference, disciplined the private sphere too.[7]

Such a discourse about *superstitio* might have remained at the level of observation, and perhaps literary denunciation of religious deviance; but in the years after the fall of the Republic – here again I follow Harriet Flower's periodization[8] – this was held to be insufficient. There had previously been

---

[6] For the behaviour to be expected of citizens in other fields for democratic Athens see Christ 2006.
[7] See Anderson and Calhoun 2008.
[8] Flower 2010.

banishments of particular religious "technicians", but now a restrictive law of associations came into being, its implementation affecting followers of Isis as well as local Lares cults.[9] All these measures were not enacted under the rubric of religious legislation: there is evidence neither of such a general emphasis nor of an explicit focus merely on religion.[10] In the situation that arose, the concern was rather to systematize indigenous Roman religion, and, first of all, to attempt to define and document it. In terms of their semantics, neither Varro nor Cicero had exclusion as their priority. Their foremost concern was the safeguarding of their own tradition. The strategy was an intellectual one: to reformulate religion as knowledge. Also pivotal was the approach taken to that tradition by each of these two authors. Varro emphasized the contingency of the tradition: an argument conducted purely on the basis of natural philosophy might lead to other, clearer solutions for worshipping the gods. Cicero, arguing directly on the basis of natural law, criticized distortions of his tradition, such as the worship of vices. He did not call a formal halt to the evolution of tradition; but, in reality, his constant recourse to the duration of a custom for its legitimation left no room for the new. In *De natura deorum* – citing Greece as his example! – he would point to the inflationary increase in the numbers of the gods as a fundamental problem.

Cicero's adoption of the law and statutes as his chosen genre reveals his political interest, and especially his interest in a programme of reform;[11] this is merely underlined by the fact that he failed to publish his treatise: with the development of the Civil War, he lost the political basis for promulgating his constitution. His choice also made it clear that he would not be satisfied with a mere description of *superstitio*. The systematic legalism of his approach is so precise in the norms it lays down that it opens the prospect of sanctions, even if these are made explicit only in a few instances in *De legibus*. Such a description of religious deviance makes it possible to envisage its criminalization.

A possible model for the Imperial age

How to characterize developments in the Imperial age against the background described so far? First it must be stressed that the work of Varro became established as standard, and was instrumental in intensifying

---

[9] On the compital cults of the first century BCE see Flambard 1981.
[10] See Ascon. *Corn.* p. 75 Clark; Bendlin 2005, 88–93.
[11] Thus Rawson 1973.

scholarly discourse about religion. But the text was not supplemented and kept up to date by later copyists, or by any editors. Not even the genre of the *Antiquitates rerum diuinarum* was perpetuated. Rather, Varro's etymological method, which he had propagated in *De lingua Latina* (with frequent reference to *Antiquitates*), was taken up as a tool for the understanding of contemporary religion.[12] Cicero's *Laws*, so far as can be established, not having been formally published in his lifetime, did not find what would still be a very limited readership until Late Antiquity:[13] at the same time as religious deviance was being prosecuted on an enormous scale.

There was no single, coherent solution under the Principate either, or any deliberate religious policy in a comprehensive sense. Research undertaken during the last decade (and, of course, I am thinking especially here of the programme Roman Imperial and Provincial Religion)[14] has established that there can be no question of either a politically devised Imperial religion or even a centrally managed, universally implemented Imperial cult.[15] Conceptualization of the Empire itself remained inadequate in vital areas of the law, for instance in respect of land law with its implications for religious law. Accordingly, it was the task of local provincial legislators and legal practitioners to establish categories analogous to those existing in the city of Rome.[16]

The rules for Roman colonies and *municipia*, the earliest version of which is to be found in the *lex Ursonensis*, provide clear indications respecting the conceptualization of religious law. These rules received brief analysis in Chapter 5.[17] The conclusion arrived at there was that regulation was confined to a small category of religion where interference with administrative structures was a danger. An appropriate apparatus of *sacerdotes publici* was provided for this category, as well as procedures for defining a calendar of festivals. Rules with regard to cults were confined, in the case of Urso, to the Capitoline Triad and the cult of Venus favoured by the colony's founder, and in the Flavian municipal laws mainly to the cult of the imperial

---

[12] See Schröter 1963.
[13] On the reception history: P. L. Schmidt 1969.
[14] Rüpke 2007d, 2014a; Cancik and Rüpke 2009a.
[15] See esp. Cancik and Rüpke 1997, 2009; Ando 2000; Cancik and Hitzl 2003; Rüpke 2007c.
[16] Cf. Gaius, *Inst.* 2.7a: *Quod in provinciis non ex auctoritate populi Romani consecratum est, proprie sacrum non est, tamen pro sacro habetur,* with Pliny, *Epistle* 10.50 (Trajan). The Babatha Archive from the province of Arabia has shown how quickly Roman norms regarding landownership came into use in the provinces under the edict of the provincial governor (I am grateful to Richard Gordon for pointing this out).
[17] *Lex: ILS* 6087.

family. Gellius in the second century even laments the lack of clear rules to ensure the Roman character of colonies.[18] A broad area of religion thus remained unregulated, and neither privileged nor forbidden.[19]

With this intrinsically minimal definition of public religion, comprising for the most part procedural rules relating to public officials, public money, and honorific positions, the scope for legally significant deviance in the religious sphere becomes very restricted. In respect of the law, at least, the principle was: what is not forbidden is allowed. The paucity of the content of this definition of *sacra publica* may be gleaned from the great number, and wide distribution, of dedications to Jupiter Optimus Maximus and – to a much greater extent – Juno and Minerva, the other members of the Capitoline Triad. The flexibility of the rules can be seen not least in the fact that one colony could get by for a century without either a temple of this triad or a *capitolium*.[20]

Alongside this minimal definition of public religion, the ruler cult contributed a degree of coherence and at the same time an element of mobility. Like no other god,[21] the Augustus of the moment, even prior to his death and official consecration as Divus Augustus (or Claudius or Vespasianus etc.), made plausible the supra-regional identity and presence of gods whose representation and cult were otherwise primarily local.[22] Finds such as the large series of marble statues from Chiragan in south-western Gaul,[23] with their likenesses of children, wives, and emperors at different times of life, show the speed and precision with which this presence was disseminated in the medium of the statue, as well as in the miniaturized form of coins.

The interplay of a narrowly based public religion and the cult of living and deified emperors can also be detected in another medium, that of calendars. With their *feriae* and temple foundation dates (*dies natales templorum*), their presence as a medium of religious memory had been increasing since the beginning of the second century BCE. But it was Caesar's calendar reform of 46 BCE that brought the graphic form of the annual calendar, the *fasti*, a popularity that led to the marble calendars of the age of Augustus and Tiberius, some of which were enormous.[24] At first, these recorded in great detail the traditional religion of

[18] Gell. *NA* 16.13.9, see Ando 2007, 432.
[19] See Rüpke 2006c and 2006d.
[20] See the example of Capua (Suet. *Tib.* 40) cited by Ando 2007, 433–4; Belayche 2001, 108–219.
[21] Ando 2000, passim; 2008, 119.
[22] Ando 2008, 56–7.
[23] Martre-Tolosane, Haute-Garonne; in the Musée Saint-Raymond des Antiques in Toulouse.
[24] Rüpke 2003, 2011b; cf. Feeney 2007.

the city of Rome, especially the new foundation festivals for the many temple restorations.[25] To this extent, they perpetuated Varro's project of an encyclopaedic portrayal of Roman religion, within the confines of the ritual agenda and generic form of the Roman festive calendar and the *fasti*. But calendars were soon dominated by the growing number of imperial festivals, with their comprehensive historical notes ("because on this day this member of X imperial house performed that action Y"), as instanced by the Tiberian *Fasti Amiterni*. This development had medium-related implications: marble was not an appropriate material on which to represent the rapid growth of imperial festivals, not to speak of the prompt erasures necessitated by a change of reign. The content of the later texts, especially the *Fasti porticus*[26] from the city of Rome and the *Feriale Duranum*, the Severan list of military festivals of the garrison in Mesopotamia,[27] shows the domination of the calendar by the accumulated festivals of the great dynasties: Augustus, Vespasian, the adoptive emperors, contemporary rulers. The festival calendar was adapted to serve the needs of an empire.[28]

Complementing the process already described, whereby regulation was concentrated in only a few areas of religious practice involving political functions, there arose a growing category of non-political religion, analogous to elite practices in the classical Greek poleis, especially the Dionysian and Orphic cults.[29] The increasing depoliticization of the public realm, to be seen above all in the more recently founded cities of the Roman Empire,[30] again played its part, encouraging a "privatization" of religion. As has already been established, however, to describe the situation that emerged in terms of an opposition between "public" and "private" would be insufficient. Factors that gave rise to a religious domain that, without being "public" in the administrative sense, was increasingly robust and highly visible, included: new foundations of associations,[31] either approved or actual; the stabilization of immigrant networks by the founding of cults; the quasi-deification of members of the economic elite by means of highly individualized divine epithets;[32] the revival or transference of sites

[25] On changes of date occasioned by restorations see Galinsky 2007, 73.
[26] Rüpke 1995, 86–90; 2011a, 142–5.
[27] *P. Dura* 54 = Fink 1971 (RMR), no. 117.
[28] For details see Stern 2012.
[29] Only briefly treated in Burkert 1977 (2nd edn 2011, Engl. tr. 1985); Bremmer 2002; Graf and Johnston 2007.
[30] See Bendlin 1997.
[31] See the contributions in Rüpke 2007e for the "third space" of associations.
[32] See Rüpke 2014a, 27–32.

of healing cults and oracles; participation in local cults, or their modification, by the military and administrative elite and merchants, in the course of their empire-wide activities and thus their putting down of roots; and, last but not least, the maintenance of supra-regional literary communication by intellectuals.

Under the conditions described, of a democratized aristocratic moral code and – since the *Constitutio Antoniniana* of 212 CE – universalized citizenship in a technical as well as a moral sense, extending to all free inhabitants of the Roman Empire, this new religious domain evolved autonomously, and in ways not dependent on legal forms. Using methods of philosophical criticism and debate,[33] to which we owe the apologetic works written by those Jews who eventually even described themselves as Christians and by other followers of Jesus, and the attacks of figures such as Celsus, it also operated through social observation expressed in satirical form, from Juvenal's *Saturae* to Lucian's *Pseudoprophetes Alexandros*. Its presence is apparent in the philosophically motivated *superstitio* discourse pursued by the likes of Seneca and Plutarch, and it did not flinch from criticizing its own public religious traditions,[34] at least in this same discourse.[35] It eventually culminated in a discourse of exclusion argued in universalizing terms: human sacrifice is barbarous; groups who practise incendiarism, incest, and cannibalism are driven by *odium humani generis*, "hatred of the human race".[36] It was not until this point that urbane criticism turned to criminalization. The criminal law has its place, of course, everywhere that property, life, or limb is endangered (*maleficium*), or where the accumulation of knowledge might be preparatory to a political coup (*diuinatio*, *curiositas*). That religious forms might be employed in committing such outrages is no excuse, and does not count as a mitigating circumstance.

Religious individuation

It is time to turn to an analysis of the processes by which norms are formulated and thus deviance defined, taking the individual as our point of

---

[33] See Attridge 1978.
[34] Lausberg (1970, 225–6) has convincingly argued that Min. Fel. 24.11 builds on Seneca's *De superstitione*; if that were the case, the senatorial and equestrian priesthoods of the *Salii* and *Luperci* would be the targets of ridicule here. She is correct in determining that Seneca went particularly far in his criticism of the public cult (Lausberg 1989, 1896).
[35] On Seneca see Setaioli 2007, 357. The same point is emphasized in Plutarch's case by Bowden 2008, 64.
[36] Tac. *Ann.* 15.44.4 (see Keresztes 1979, 253–5, with whom I do not, however, concur in this instance); cf. Plin. *Ep.* 10.49.

departure. How did the religious context outlined for the period of the end of the Republic, and cited in respect of the statutes of the fourth century, influence the various degrees and types of individuality achieved by different people involved in processes of individuation?

Individuation is inseparably linked to socialization.[37] How does a person become a fully-fledged member of society? And how does he or she become a fully functioning autonomous adult? Both questions relate to the same process, and naturally entail a multitude of possible ways of addressing social functionality and personal autonomy. Any desirable outcome of such a process is, self-evidently, predicated on a normative statement.

There were many variants of this process in the societies of the ancient Mediterranean world. Even the basic level of socialization in the primal social group of the family was full of complications. One had in principle to learn roles that varied according to biographical status: that of son, elder sister, wife, *pater familias*. But families were not stable. The maternal death rate, both direct and indirect, was high; military conflict, endemic to the Mediterranean basin, might also lead to the death or enslavement of males.[38] Processes of urbanization increased social and geographical mobility. As I have already shown, migration was a frequent phenomenon. Secondary socialization, implemented by specialists or by institutions, was presumably restricted to a minority of wealthy people, and almost exclusively to male members of that group. By this means, individuals might receive an education that went beyond the writing of their own name, or the reading of a brief inscription.[39] Bilingualism was common among members of local elites of non-Greek or non-Roman origin.[40] In brief, there were many possible modalities of de-traditionalization (involving either altered behaviour or simply reflection on, and choice of, "the old ways"), which I take as a fundamental indicator of individuality.

What is to be said about religious individuation and its changing face? My analyses so far have indicated some areas where that process of change may be observed. When recourse was had to the shifting apparatus of norms, it was with a view to perfection, not to judgement for judgement's

---

[37] For the concept of individuation see Rüpke 2013c; Rosenberger 2013b.
[38] On this last point see now Eckstein 2008. Ancient demography: Scheidel 2001.
[39] For discussion of this point see Harris 1989 and Bowman and Woolf 1994. See also Johnson 2013; Woolf 2013.
[40] For the cultural implications see Romaine 1989; for the development in the East see Cotton 2009.

sake. Imperial age imagery (the emperor performing a libation at the altar), the sacred idylls to be found in private murals and dedicatory reliefs, but above all the multitude of votive inscriptions, may have had an important mediating role, while at the same time revealing the (economically contingent) contexts of competing modes of behaviour.

Influences favouring detraditionalization may have operated at a comparable level of religious practice: the differentiation of what tended to be a narrow spectrum[41] of "public" religion, and the emphasis of obligation on the imperial cult, may have thrown into relief the elective character of the broader area of religious activity. This was nothing fundamentally new. The individual's competency to identify the right god for the right occasion is characteristic of advanced polytheism.[42] At the same time, urban conditions favoured the development of a different form of "heretical imperative" (Peter L. Berger), or impulse to make a conscious choice, than existed within the scope of an all-purpose rural sanctuary.[43]

Hand in hand with the process just mentioned went an increase in religious options, rarely exclusive, often on only an occasional basis. Mobility played an especially significant role here: for Roman citizens in the provinces it had the effect of turning their efforts to maintain Italian traditions, typically involving error-prone attempts to reproduce familiar religious practices under the new local conditions, into decisions that, locally, signified membership of one of the central cultures of the Roman Empire; it had an analogous effect for immigrants to Rome, at least for those joining other members of the same ethnic group; in each case, available local options increased rapidly, at least in the second or third generation, both by processes of acculturation and by the attractive power of the god from far-off climes.[44] The way was thus opened for personal differentiation, to be followed rapidly by competition in terms of financial engagement.

Since Varro's *Antiquitates* and Virgil's *Aeneid*, the availability of religion in Latin texts had encouraged reflection on its nature. Sufficient evidence for this is provided by the reception of Varro in Ovid's commentary on

---

[41] Individually, however, these cults could be highly complex, as can be seen in the case of the *feriale* of the Ceres cult at Carthage (Ennabli and Scheid 2008; cf. Ennabli 1999 and Ando 2007, 435).

[42] Gladigow 2005, 141–2.

[43] The specifics of rural religion in antiquity are still poorly understood: Burns and Eadie 2001; Steinsapir 2005; Auffarth 2009; Stek 2009.

[44] See the case studies in Rüpke 2014a.

the calendar, dating from the Augustan period *(Libri fastorum),*[45] and by the interest shown in Virgil's religious aetiology.[46]

Finally, religious choice itself might be biographically embodied. A permanent link with a deity and the creation of a corresponding epithet or device, with particular emphasis on Venus, had already been a mark of late Republican military commanders.[47] Virgil's epic presents us with just such a permanent option – and no longer as problematically as in Euripides' *Hippolytus* – in the connection between Aeneas and Venus. Religion became an important component and token of character in Suetonius' biographies of emperors, and constitutes the central biographical experience in Apuleius' *Metamorphoses* and Aelius Aristides' *Hieroi logoi.* These central processes in individual lives did not conflict with the minimal core of public religion. As reflected both externally, in biography, and internally, in autobiography (even when fictitious), religion became a personal attribute that, while demonstrating individuality, at the same time attested to successful socialization.

Only rarely in this context do we discover deviance. As became apparent in the case of Apuleius, deviance was something to be denied where suspicion of criminality was concerned. Deviance is primarily identified where the boundary between religious activity and the denunciation of power as illegitimate was crossed; divination was the classic case in Imperial historiography. Where religion becomes knowledge, ignorance and error are also possibilities. Philosophical groups appear to have dealt with this problem defensively, by embracing traditionalism in their religious activities rather than radical solutions. Augustine was to diagnose and reject this laissez-faire style of dealing with religious variations in the introduction to his treatise *On True Religion.* It was only with the normalization of religious knowledge, as undertaken in the late fourth century, that alternative bodies of knowledge became generally problematic. Even before this time, however, radical movements that turned individual decisions such as conversion into a life choice might turn out to be problematic if they conflicted with the minimal consensual core. The problem was rendered more acute by the fact that this core of obligatory religion constantly grew after the third century, not least – although also, perhaps, not primarily[48] – because it was used ever more intensively to legitimate imperial rule and succession. In

---

[45] On the genre see Rüpke 1994, 2009c.
[46] Binder 1988; Orlin 2007.
[47] See Sauron 1994.
[48] Kahlos 2009 has revisited this classic theme of the growth of religious intolerance through monocratic use of religion, with a preference for monotheistic religion, in the legitimation of rule.

these conditions of expanding religious normalization, religious individuality easily became deviance, to the extent that it might be preferable to flee into the desert, or, conversely, into the complex role of a bishop. The latter option was not open to Manicheans and Jews. And it was the pleasure of heresiographs and legislators during the following centuries continually to lengthen this list of exceptions and deviances.

References

Abernetty, Gualteros 1911. *De Plutarchi qui fertur de superstitione libello.* Diss. Königsberg.

Anderson, Leon and Calhoun, Thomas H. 2008. "Strategies for Researching Street Deviance." In: Thio, A., Calhoun, T. H., and Conyers, A. (eds), *Readings in Deviant Behavior.* Boston, MA: Pearson. 18–23.

Ando, Clifford 2000. *Imperial Ideology and Provincial Loyalty in the Roman Empire.* Berkeley, CA: University of California Press.

    2001. "Signs, Idols, and the Incarnation in Augustinian Metaphysics." In: *Representations* 73. 24–53.

    2006. "Religion and ius publicum." In: Ando, Clifford and Rüpke, Jörg (eds), *Religion and Law in Classical and Christian Rome.* Potsdamer altertumswissenschaftliche Beiträge 15. Stuttgart: Steiner. 126–45.

    2007. "Exporting Roman Religion." In: Rüpke, Jörg (ed.), *The Blackwell Companion to Roman Religion.* Oxford: Blackwell. 429–45.

    2008. *The Matter of the Gods: Religion and the Roman Empire.* Berkeley, CA: University of California Press.

Ando, Clifford and Rüpke, Jörg (eds) 2006. "Introduction." In: *Religion and Law in Classical and Christian Rome.* Potsdamer altertumswissenschaftliche Beiträge 15. Stuttgart: Steiner. 9–13.

André, Jean-Marie 1983. "Sénèque théologien: l'évolution de sa pensée jusqu'au 'De superstitione'." In: *Helmantica* 34. 55–71.

Annus, Amar (ed.) 2010. *Divination and Interpretation of Signs in the Ancient World,* Oriental institute seminars 6. Chicago, IL: Oriental Institute of the University of Chicago.

Athanassiadi, Polymnia and Frede, Michael 1999. *Pagan Monotheism in Late Antiquity.* Oxford: Clarendon Press.

Attridge, Harold W. 1978. "The Philosophical Critique of Religion under the Early Empire." In: *Aufstieg und Niedergang der römischen Welt* 2.16.1. 45–78.

Auffarth, Christoph (ed.) 2009. *Religion auf dem Lande: Entstehung und Veränderung von Sakrallandschaften unter römischer Herrschaft.* Potsdamer altertumswissenschaftliche Beiträge 28. Stuttgart: Steiner.

Bäbler, Balbina and Nesselrath, Heinz-Günther 2006. *Ars et Verba. Die Kunstbeschreibung des Kallistratos. Einführung, Text, Übersetzung, Anmerkungen, archäologischer Kommentar.* Munich: Saur.

Bailey, Michael D. 2007. *Magic and Superstition in Europe: A Concise History from Antiquity to the Present*. Lanham, MD: Rowman & Littlefield.

Balch, David L. 2008. *Roman Domestic Art and Early House Churches*. Tübingen: Mohr Siebeck.

Baldassarri, Maria 1996. "Inquadramento filosofico del De superstitione Plutarcheo." In: Gallo, Italo (ed.), *Plutarco e la religione*. Naples: D'Auria. 373–87.

Barceló, Pedro 2013. *Das römische Reich im religiösen Wandel der Spätantike: Kaiser und Bischöfe im Widerstreit*. Regensburg: Pustet.

Barchiesi, Alessandro 2006. "Mobilità e religione nell' Eneide: Diaspora, culto, spazio, identità locali." In: Elm von der Osten, Dorothee, Rüpke, Jörg, and Waldner, Katharina (eds), *Texte als Medium und Reflexion von Religion im römischen Reich*. Potsdamer altertumswissenschaftliche Beiträge 14. Stuttgart: Steiner. 7–12.

Bauer, Franz Alto 2007. "Virtuelle Statuensammlungen." In: Bauer, Franz Alto and Witschel, Christian (eds), *Statuen in der Spätantike*. Wiesbaden: Reichert. 79–109.

Bayet, Jean 1957. *Histoire politique et psychologique de la religion romain*. Paris: Payot.

Beard, Mary, North, John, and Price, Simon 1998. *Religions of Rome. 1: A History. 2: A Sourcebook*. Cambridge: Cambridge University Press.

Beer, Cecilia 1987. "Comparative Votive Religion: The Evidence of Children in Cyprus, Greece and Etruria." In: Linders, Tullia and Gullög, Nordquist (eds), *Gifts to the Gods: Proceedings of the Uppsala Symposium 1985*. Uppsala: Universitet. 21–9.

Belardi, Walter 1976. *Superstitio*. Rome: Istituto di Glottologia, Università di Roma.

Belayche, Nicole 2001. *Iudaea-Palaestina: The Pagan Cults in Roman Palestine (Second to Fourth Century)*. Tübingen: Mohr Siebeck.

2011. "Entre deux éclats de rire: Sacrifice et représentation du divin dans le 'De sacrificiis' de Lucien." In: Delforge, V. P. and Prescendi, F. (eds), *"Nourrir les dieux?" Sacrifice et représentation du divin*. Liège: Centre Internationale d'Étude de la Religion Grecque Antique. 165–80.

Belayche, Nicole et al. 2005. "Divination romaine." In: *ThesCRA* 3. 79–104.

Belayche, Nicole and Rüpke, Jörg 2007. "Divination et révélation dans les mondes grec et romain: Présentation." In: *Revue de l'histoire des religions* 224.2. 139–47.

Belting, Hans 1990. *Bild und Kult: Eine Geschichte des Bildes vor dem Zeitalter der Kunst*. Munich: Beck.

2007. *Bilderfragen: Die Bildwissenschaften im Aufbruch*. Munich: Fink.

Bendlin, Andreas 1997. "Peripheral Centres – Central Peripheries: Religious Communication in the Roman Empire." In: Cancik, Hubert and Rüpke, Jörg (eds), *Römische Reichsreligion und Provinzialreligion*. Tübingen: Mohr Siebeck. 35–68.

2005. "'Eine Zusammenkunft um der *religio* willen ist erlaubt …?' Zu den politischen und rechtlichen Konstruktionen von (religiöser) Vergemeinschaftung." In: Kippenberg, Hans G. and Schuppert, Gunnar Folke (eds), *Die verrechtlichte Religion: Der Öffentlichkeitsstatus von Religionsgemeinschaften*. Tübingen: Mohr Siebeck. 65–107.

Beutler, Christian 1982. *Statua: Die Entstehung der nachantiken Statue und der europäische Individualismus*. Munich: Prestel.

Binder, Gerhard (ed.) 1988. *Saeculum Augustum 2: Religion und Literatur*. Wege der Forschung 512. Darmstadt: Wissenschaftliche Buchgesellschaft.

Bispham, Edward and Smith, Christopher (eds) 2000. *Religion in Archaic and Republican Rome and Italy: Evidence and Experience*. Edinburgh: Edinburgh University Press.

Bouma, Jelle 1996. *Religio votiva: The Archaeology of Latial Votive Religion: 5th–3rd c. BC*. 3 vols. Doctoral thesis: Groningen.

Bourdieu, Pierre 1972. *Esquisse d'une théorie de la pratique, précédé de trois études d'ethnologie kabyle*. Geneva: Droz S.A.

1998. *Practical Reason: On the Theory of Action*. Cambridge: Polity Press.

Bowden, Hugh 2008. "Before Superstition and After: Theophrastus and Plutarch on Deisidaimonia." In: Smith, S. A. and Knight, Alan (eds), *The Religion of Fools? Superstition Past and Present*. Past and Present Supplement 3. Oxford: Oxford University Press. 56–71.

Bowes, Kimberly D. 2007. "'Christianization' and the Rural Home." In: *Journal of Early Christian Studies* 15.2. 143–70.

Bowman, Alan K. and Woolf, Greg (eds) 1994. *Literacy and Power in the Ancient World*. Cambridge: Cambridge University Press.

Boyarin, Daniel 2003. "Semantic Differences; or, 'Judaism'/'Christianity'." In: Becker, Adam and Reed, Annette Yoshiko (eds), *The Ways that Never Parted: Jews and Christians in Late Antiquity and the Early Middle Ages*. Texts and Studies in Ancient Judaism / Texte und Studien zum Antiken Judentum 95. Tübingen: Mohr Siebeck. 65–85.

2004a. *Border Lines: The Partition of Judaeo-Christianity*. Divinations. Rereading Late Ancient Religion. Philadelphia, PA: University of Pennsylvania Press.

2004b. "The Christian Invention of Judaism: The Theodosian Empire and the Rabbinic Refusal of Religion." In: *Representations* 85. 21–57.

2006. "Twenty-Four Refutations: Continuing the Conversations." In: *Henoch: Studies in Judaism and Christianity from Second Temple to Late Antiquity* 28.1. 30–45.

Bräunlein, Peter J. 2009. "Ikonische Repräsentation von Religion." In: Kippenberg, Hans G., Rüpke, Jörg, and Stuckrad, Kocku von (eds), *Europäische Religionsgeschichte*, Vol. 2. Göttingen: Vandenhoeck & Ruprecht. 771–810.

Bredekamp, Horst 2010. *Theorie des Bildakts*. Frankfurt am Main: Suhrkamp.

Bremmer, Jan N. 2002. *The Rise and Fall of the Afterlife*. The 1995 Read-Tuckwell Lectures at the University of Bristol. London: Routledge.

Brenk, F. E. 1977. *In Mist Apparelled: Religious Themes in Plutarch's Moralia and Lives.* Mnemosyne Supplements 48. Leiden: Brill.

Burkert, Walter 1977. *Griechische Religion der archaischen und klassischen Epoche.* Stuttgart: Kohlhammer.

1985 [1987]. *Greek Religion: Archaic and Classical.* Oxford: Blackwell.

Burns, Thomas S. and Eadie, John W. 2001. *Urban Centers and Rural Contexts in Late Antiquity.* East Lansing, MI: Michigan State University Press.

Burrus, Virginia et al. 2006. "Boyarin's Work: A Critical Assessment." In: *Henoch* 28. 7–30.

Cancik, Hubert 1995. "Militia perennis: Typologie und Theologie der Kriege Roms gegen Veji bei T. Livius." In: Stietencron, Heinrich von and Rüpke, Jörg (eds), *Töten im Krieg.* Veröffentlichungen des Instituts für Historische Anthropologie 6. Freiburg: Alber. 197–212.

1998. *Antik – modern: Beiträge zur römischen und deutschen Kulturgeschichte.* Stuttgart: Metzler.

2003. *Verse und Sachen: Kulturwissenschaftliche Interpretationen römischer Dichtung.* Würzburg: Königshausen & Neumann.

2006. " 'Götter einführen': Ein myth-historisches Modell für die Diffusion von Religion in Vergils Aeneis." In: Elm von der Osten, Dorothee, Rüpke, Jörg, and Waldner, Katharina (eds), *Texte als Medium und Reflexion von Religion im Römischen Reich.* Potsdamer altertumswissenschaftliche Beiträge 14. Stuttgart: Steiner. 31–40.

Cancik, Hubert (eds) 2009. *Die Religion des Imperium Romanum: Koine und Konfrontationen.* Tübingen: Mohr Siebeck.

Cancik, Hubert and Hitzl, Konrad (eds) 2003. *Die Praxis der Herrscherverehrung in Rom und seinen Provinzen.* Tübingen: Mohr Siebeck.

Cancik, Hubert and Rüpke, Jörg (eds) 1997. *Römische Reichsreligion und Provinzialreligion.* Tübingen: Mohr Siebeck.

Cardauns, Burkhart 1976. *M. Terentius Varro, Antiquitates rerum divinarum. 1: Die Fragmente. 2: Kommentar* (Akademie der Wissenschaften und der Literatur, Mainz, *Abhandlungen der Geistes- und sozialwissenschaftlichen Klasse* 1). Wiesbaden: Steiner.

Certeau, Michel de 1988. *The Writing of History.* Tr. by Tom Conley. New York, NY: Columbia University Press.

2007. *Arts de Faire.* New edn by Luce Giard. Paris: Gallimard (Engl. *The Practice of Everyday Life.* Tr. by Steven Randall. Berkeley, CA: University of California Press, 1984, repr. 2011).

Christ, Matthew R. 2006. *The Bad Citizen in Classical Athens.* Cambridge: Cambridge University Press.

Clark, Anna 2007. *Divine Qualities: Cult and Community in Republican Rome.* Oxford: Oxford University Press.

Clark, Gillian 2005. *Christianity and Roman Society.* Cambridge: Cambridge University Press.

Clarke, John R. 1998. *Looking at Lovemaking: Constructions of Sexuality in Roman Art 100 BC – AD 250.* Los Angeles, CA: University of California Press.

2003. *Art in the Lives of Ordinary Romans: Visual Representation and Non-Elite Viewers in Italy, 100* BC – AD *315*. Berkeley, CA: University of California Press.

2007. *Looking at Laughter: Humor, Power, and Transgression in Roman Visual Culture, 100* BC – AD *250*. Berkeley, CA: University of California Press.

Cole, Susan Guettel 2004. *Landscapes, Gender and Ritual Space: The Ancient Greek Experience*. The Joan Palevsky Imprint in Classical Literature. Berkeley, CA: University of California Press.

Connolly, Serena 2010. *Lives behind the Laws: The World of the Codex Hermogenianus*. Bloomington, IN: Indiana University Press.

Cotton, Hannah 2009. *From Hellenism to Islam: Cultural and Linguistic Change in the Roman Near East*. Cambridge: Cambridge University Press.

Cramer, Fredrick H. 1954. *Astrology in Roman Law and Politics*. Memoirs of the American Philosophical Society 37. Philadelphia, PA: American Philosophical Society.

Crang, Mike 1997. "Picturing Practices: Research through the Tourist Gaze." *Progress in Human Geography* 21. 359–73.

Crawford, Michael H. (ed.) 1996. *Roman Statutes*. Bulletin of the Institute of Classical Studies, Suppl. 64. London: Institute of Classical Studies.

Creed, John 1084. *Lactantius, De mortibus persecutorum*. Oxford: Clarendon Press.

Cristofani, Mauro 1987. "I santuari: tradizioni decorative." In: Cristofani, Mauro (ed.), *Etruria e Lazio arcaico: Atti dell'incontro di studio (10–11 novembre 1986)*. Quaderni del centro di Studio per l'archeologia etrusco-italica 15. Rome: Consiglio nazionale delle ricerche. 95–120.

Cusamano, Nicola et al. (eds) 2013. *Memory and Religious Experience in the Graeco-Roman World*. Potsdamer altertumswissenschaftliche Beiträge 45. Stuttgart: Steiner.

De Souza, Manuel 2011. "Une inversion de la norme religieuse à la fin de la République." In: Cabouret, Bernadette and Charles-Laforge, Marie-Odile (eds), *La norme religieuse dans l'antiquité*. Paris: De Boccard. 25–36.

Delmaire, Roland 2005. *Les lois religieuses des empereurs romains de Constantin à Théodose II: Code théodosien livre XVI*. Paris: Cerf.

Dohrmann, Natalie B. and Reed, Annette Yoshiko (eds) 2013. *Jews, Christians, and the Roman Empire*. Jewish Culture and Contexts. Philadelphia, PA: University of Pennsylvania Press.

Dunand, Francoise 2013. "Images de dieux en dialogue." In: Bricault, Laurent and Bonnet, Corinne (eds), *Panthée: Religious Transformations in the Graeco-Roman Empire*. Religions in the Graeco-Roman World 177. Leiden: Brill. 191–232.

Dyck, Andrew R. 2004. *A Commentary on Cicero 'De legibus'*. Ann Arbor, MI: Michigan University Press.

Eckstein, Arthur M. 2008. *Rome Enters the Greek East: From Anarchy to Hierarchy in the Hellenistic Mediterranean, 230–170* BC. Malden, MA: Blackwell.

Eich, Peter 2011. *Gottesbild und Wahrnehmung: Studien zu Ambivalenzen früher griechischer Götterdarstellungen (ca. 800 v.Chr. – ca. 400 v.Chr.)*. Potsdamer altertumswissenschaftliche Beiträge 34. Stuttgart: Steiner.

Eidinow, Esther 2007. *Oracles, Curses, and Risk among the Ancient Greeks.* Oxford: Oxford University Press.

2011. "Networks and Narratives: A Model for Ancient Greek Religion." In: *Kernos* 24. 9–38.

2013. "Oracular Consultation, Fate, and the Concept of the Individual." In: Rosenberger, Veit (ed.), *Divination in the Ancient World: Religious Options and the Individual.* Potsdamer altertumswissenschaftliche Beiträge 46. Stuttgart: Steiner. 21–39.

Eitrem, Samuel 1955. "Zur Deisidämonie." In: *Symbolae Osloenses* 31. 155–69.

Engels, David 2008. *Das römische Vorzeichenwesen (753–27 v. Chr.): Quellen, Terminologie, Kommentar, historische Entwicklung.* Potsdamer altertumswissenschaftliche Beiträge 22. Stuttgart: Steiner.

Ennabli, Liliane 1999. "A propos de Mégara." In: Lancel, Serge (ed.), *Numismatique, langues, écritures et arts du livre, spécificité des arts figurés.* Afrique du Nord antique et médiévale. Paris: Éditions du Comité des Travaux Historiques et Scientifiques. 193–210.

Ennabli, Liliane and Scheid, John 2008. "Une lex sacra de Carthage relative au culte des Cereres? Nouvelles observations sur les fragments découverts dans la basilique de Carthagenna." In: *Rendiconti Pontificia Accademia Romana di Archeologia* 80. 37–75.

Erbse, Hartmut 1952. "Plutarchs Schrift PERI DEISIDAIMONIAS." In: *Hermes* 80. 296–314.

Estienne, Sylvia 2010. "Simulacra deorum versus ornamenta aedium: The Status of Divine Images in the Temples of Rome." In: Mylonopoulos, Joannis (ed.), *Divine Images and Human Imaginations in Ancient Greece and Rome.* Leiden: Brill. 257–71.

Faraone, Chris 2011. "Text, Image and Medium: The Evolution of Graeco-Roman Magical Gemstones." In: Entwistle, Chris and Adams, Noel (eds), *'Gems of Heaven': Recent Research on Engraved Gemstones in Late Antiquity ca.* AD *200–600.* British Museum Research Publications 177. Oxford: The British Museum Press. 50–61.

Faraone, Chris and Naiden, F. S. (eds) 2012. *Greek and Roman Animal Sacrifice: Ancient Victims, Modern Observers.* Cambridge: Cambridge University Press.

Feeney, Denis 2007. *Caesar's Calendar: Ancient Time and the Beginnings of History.* Sather Classical Lectures. Berkeley, CA: University of California Press.

Ferri, Giorgio 2010. *Tutela urbis: Il significato e la concezione della divinità tutelare cittadina nella religione romana.* Potsdamer altertumswissenschaftliche Beiträge 32. Stuttgart: Steiner.

Flambard, Jean-Marc 1981. "Collegia Compitalicia: Phénomène associatif, cadres territoriaux et cadres civiques dans le monde romain à l'époque républicaine." In: *Ktema* 6. 143–66.

Flower, Harriet I. 2000. "The Tradition of the Spolia Opima: M. Claudius Marcellus and Augustus." In: *Classical Antiquity* 19. 34–64.

2003. "'Memories' of Marcellus: History and Memory in Roman Republican Culture." In: Eigler, Ulrich (ed.), *Formen römischer Geschichtsschreibung von den Anfängen bis Livius: Gattungen, Autoren, Kontexte*. Darmstadt: Wissenschaftliche Buchgesellschaft. 39–52.

2010. *Roman Republics*. Princeton, NJ: Princeton University Press.

Fögen, Marie-Theres 1993. *Die Enteignung der Wahrsager: Studien zum kaiserlichen Wissensmonopol in der Spätantike*. Frankfurt am Main: Suhrkamp.

Fonrobert, Charlotte Elisheva 2013. "'Humanity was Created as an Individual': Synechdocal Individuality in the Mishnah as a Jewish Response to Romanization." In: Rüpke, Jörg (ed.), *The Individual in the Religions of the Ancient Mediterranean*. Oxford: Oxford University Press. 489–521.

Fowler, Chris 2013. "Identities in Transformation: Identities, Funerary Rites and the Mortuary Process." In: Tarlow, Sarah and Stutz, Liv Nilsson (eds), *The Oxford Handbook of the Archaeology of Death and Burial*. Oxford: Oxford University Press. 511–26.

Frakes, Robert M. 2011. *Compiling the Collatio legum Mosaicarum et Romanarum in Late Antiquity*. Oxford: Oxford University Press.

Fredriksen, Paula 2003. "What 'Parting of the Ways'? Jews, Gentiles, and the Ancient Mediterranean City." In: Becker, Adam and Reed, Annette Yoshiko (eds), *The Ways that Never Parted: Jews and Christians in Late Antiquity and the Early Middle Ages*. Texts and Studies in Ancient Judaism / Texte und Studien zum Antiken Judentum 95. Tübingen: Mohr Siebeck. 35–63.

Fridh-Haneson, Britt Marie 1987. "Votive Terracottas from Italy: Types and Problems." In: Linders, Tullia and Nordquist, Gullög (eds), *Gifts to the Gods: Proceedings of the Uppsala Symposium 1985*. Uppsala: Universitet. 67–75.

Galinsky, Karl 2007. "Continuity and Change: Religion in the Augustan Semi-Century." In: Rüpke, J. (ed.), *A Companion to the Roman Religion*. Malden, MA: Blackwell. 71–82.

Geertz, Clifford 1966. "Religion as a Cultural System." In: Banton, Michael (ed.), *Anthropological Approaches to the Study of Religion*. London: Tavistock. 1–46.

Girardet, Klaus M. 1983. *Die Ordnung der Welt: Ein Beitrag zur philosophischen und politischen Interpretation von Ciceros Schrift de legibus*. Historia Einzelschriften 42. Wiesbaden: Steiner.

Gladigow, Burkhard 2005. *Religionswissenschaft als Kulturwissenschaft*. Stuttgart: Kohlhammer.

2008. "Opferkritik, Opferverbote und propagandistische Opfer." In: Stravrianopoulou, Eftychia, Michaels, Axel, and Ambos, Claus (eds), *Transformations in Sacrificial Practice: From Antiquity to Modern Times*. Münster: LIT. 263–87.

Goodman, Martin 2003. "Modeling the 'Parting of the Ways.'" In: Becker, Adam and Reed, Annette Yoshiko (eds), *The Ways that Never Parted: Jews and Christians in Late Antiquity and the Early Middle Ages*. Texts and Studies in Ancient Judaism / Texte und Studien zum Antiken Judentum 95. Tübingen: Mohr Siebeck. 119–29.

Görgemanns, Herwig 2003. *Plutarch: Drei religionsphilosophische Schriften.* Griechisch–deutsch. Düsseldorf: Artemis & Winkler.

Gordon, R. L. 1979. "The Real and the Imaginary: Production and Religion in the GraecoRoman World." In: *Art History* 2. 5–34.

   1990. "The Veil of Power: Emperors, Sacrificers and Benefactors." In: Beard, Mary and North, John (eds), *Pagan Priests: Religion and Power in the Ancient World.* London: Duckworth. 201–31.

   2006. "[Rev.] Martin, Dale B. 'Inventing Superstition: From the Hippocratics to the Christians 2004'." In: *Gnomon* 78. 521–6.

   2008. "Superstitio, Superstition and Religious Repression in the Late Roman Republic and Principate (100 BCE–300 CE)." In: Smith, Stephen A. and Knight, Alan (eds), *The Religion of Fools? Superstition Past and Present.* Past & Present Supplement N.S. 3. Oxford: Oxford University Press. 72–94.

Graf, Fritz 2001. "Der Eigensinn der Götterbilder in antiken religiösen Diskursen." In: Boehm, Gottfried (ed.), *Homo Pictor.* Colloquium Rauricum. Munich: Saur. 227–43.

Graf, Fritz and Johnston, Sarah Iles 2007. *Ritual Texts for the Afterlife: Orpheus and the Bacchic Gold Tablets.* London: Routledge.

Harris, William V. 1989. *Ancient Literacy.* Cambridge, MA: Harvard University Press.

Hesberg, Henner von 2004. "Dona cano divum: Ein Relief aus Köln mit der Wiedergabe eines Jägers vor einem Heiligtum der Diana." In: Gebauer, Jörg et al. (eds), *Bildergeschichte: Festschrift Klaus Stähler.* Möhnesee: Bibliopolis. 208–20.

   2007. "Die Statuengruppe im Tempel der Dioskuren von Cori: Bemerkungen zum Aufstellungskontext von Kultbildern in spätrepublikanischer Zeit." In: *Mitteilungen des Deutschen Archäologischen Instituts, Römische Abteilung* 113. 443–61.

Hoffmann, Zsuzsanna 1985–8. "Wahrsager und Wahrsagung bei Plautus." In: *Acta antiqua* 31. 367–79.

Horbury, William 1998. *Jews and Christians in Contact and Controversy.* Edinburgh: T&T Clark.

Hubbeling, Hubertus G. 1986. "Symbole als Repräsentation und Präsentation." In: Kippenberg, Hans G. and Hubbeling, Hubertus G. (eds), *Zur symbolischen Repräsentation von Religion.* Groninger Abhandlungen zu verschiedenen Symboltheorien. Berlin: de Gruyter. 1–5.

Izzet, Vedia 2001. "Tuscan Order: The Development of Etruscan Sanctuary Architecture." In: Bispham, Edward and Smith, Christopher (eds), *Religion in Archaic and Republican Rome and Italy: Evidence and Experience.* Edinburgh: Edinburgh University Press. 34–53.

Janowitz, Naomi (ed.) 2001. *Magic in the Roman World: Pagans, Jews and Christians.* Religion in the First Christian Centuries. London: Routledge.

Joas, Hans 2001. *Lehrbuch der Soziologie.* Frankfurt am Main: Campus.

Johnson, William A. 2013. "Libraries and Reading Culture in the High Empire." In: König, Jason, Oikonomopoulou, Katerina, and Woolf, Greg (eds), *Ancient Libraries.* Cambridge: Cambridge University Press. 347–63.

Jung, Matthias 2004. "Qualitative Erfahrung in Alltag, Kunst und Religion." In: Mattenklott, Gert (ed.), *Ästhetische Erfahrung im Zeichen der Entgrenzung der Künste: Epistemische, ästhetische und religiöse Erfahrungsformen im Vergleich.* Hamburg: Meiner. 31–53.

2005. "'Making us Explicit': Artikulation als Organisationsprinzip von Erfahrung." In: Schlette, Magnus (ed.), *Anthropologie der Artikulation: Begriffliche Grundlagen und transdisziplinäre Perspektiven.* Würzburg: Königshausen & Neumann. 103–41.

2006. "Making Life Explicit: The Symbolic Pregnance of Religious Experience." In: *Svensk Teologisk Kvartalskrift* 82 (Volume Ernst Cassirer). 16–23.

Kahlos, Maijastina 2009. *Forbearance and Compulsion: The Rhetoric of Religious Tolerance and Intolerance in Late Antiquity.* London: Duckworth.

Kastenmeier, Pia 2001. "Priap zum Gruße: Der Hauseingang der Casa dei Vettii in Pompeji." In: *Mitteilungen des deutschen archäologischen Instituts, Römische Abteilung* 108. 301–11.

Kearns, Emily 2011. "The Rationale of Cakes and Bloodless Offerings in Greek Sacrifice." In: Delforge, V. P. and Prescendi, F. (eds), *"Nourrir les dieux?" Sacrifice et représentation du divin.* Liège: Centre Internationale d'Étude de la Religion Grecque Antique. 89–103.

Keresztes, Paul 1979. "The Imperial Roman Government and the Christian Church: I. From Nero to the Severi." In: *Aufstieg und Niedergang der römischen Welt* II.23.1. 247–315.

Kindt, Julia 2009. "Polis Religion: A Critical Appreciation." In: *Kernos* 22. 9–34.

2012. *Rethinking Greek Religion.* Cambridge: Cambridge University Press.

Kippenberg, Hans. G. 1990. "Introduction." In: *Visible Religion* 7. vii–xix.

Kindt, Julia 1997. "Magic in Roman Civil Discourse: Why Rituals Could be Illegal." In Schäfer, Peter, and Kippenberg, Hans G. (eds), *Envisioning Magic.* Leiden: Brill. 137–63.

2005. "'Nach dem Vorbild eines öffentlichen Gemeinwesens': Diskurse römischer Juristen über private religiöse Vereinigungen." In: Kippenberg, Hans. G. and Schuppert, Gunar Folke (eds), *Die verrechtlichte Religion: Der Öffentlichkeitsstatus von Religionsgemeinschaften.* Tübingen: Mohr Siebeck. 37–63.

2009. "Religion als Geimeinschaftsgut: Religiöse Zusammenkünfte und Rituale als rechtliche Tatbestände." In: Kippenberg, Hans. G., Rüpke, Jörg, and Stuckrad, Kocku von (eds), *Europäische Religionsgeschichte*, Vol. 1. Göttingen: Vandenhoeck & Ruprecht. 127–54.

Klauck, Hans-Josef 1994. *Alte Welt und neuer Glaube: Beiträge zur Religionsgeschichte, Forschungsgeschichte und Theologie des Neuen Testaments.* Freiburg, Switzerland: Universitäts-Verlag.

Knoblauch, Hubert 1999. *Religionssoziologie.* Berlin: de Gruyter.

Kracke, Bärbel, Roux, René, and Rüpke, Jörg (eds) 2013. *Die Religion des Individuums.* Vorlesungen des Interdisziplinären Forums Religion 9. Münster: Aschendorff.

Kramer, Fritz W. 2001. "Praktiken der Imagination." In: Graevenitz, Gerhart von, Rieger, Stefan, and Thürlemann, Felix (eds), *Die Unvermeidlichkeit der Bilder.* Tübingen: Narr. 17–29.

Krasser, Helmut 2005. "Universalisierung und Identitätskonstruktion: Formen und Funktionen der Wissenskodifikation im kaiserzeitlichen Rom." In: Oesterle, Günter (ed.), *Erinnerung, Gedächtnis, Wissen: Studien zur kulturwissenschaftlichen Gedächtnisforschung.* Göttingen: Vandenhoeck & Ruprecht. 357–75.

Lafond, Yves 2009. "Normes religieuses et identité civique dans les cités de Grèce égéenne (IIe s. av. J.-C.–IIIe s. ap. J.-C.)." In: Brulé, Pierre (ed.), *La norme en matière religieuse en Grèce ancienne.* Actes du XIIe colloque international du CIERGA (Rennes, septembre 2007). Kernos Supplement 21. Liège: Kernos. 321–34.

Latte, Kurt 1960. *Römische Religionsgeschichte.* Handbuch der Altertumswissenschaft 5.4. Munich: Beck.

Lausberg, Marion 1970. "Zur Schrift De Superstitione." In: Lausberg, Marion (ed.), *Untersuchungen zu Senecas Fragmenten.* Berlin: de Gruyter. 197–227.

———— 1989. "Senecae operum fragmenta: Überblick und Forschungsbericht." In: *Aufstieg und Niedergang der römischen Welt* II.36.3. 1879–961.

Lieu, Judith, North, John, and Rajak, Tessa (eds) 1994. *The Jews among Pagans and Christians: In the Roman Empire.* London: Routledge.

Lightfoot, Jane L. 2007. "The Apology of Ps. Meliton." In: *Studi epigrafici e lingustici sul Vicino Oriente antico* 24. 59–110.

Lightstone, Jack N. 2002. *Mishnah and the Social Formation of the Early Rabbinic Guild: A Socio-Rhetorical Approach. With an Appendix by Vernon K. Robbins.* Studies in Christianity and Judaism 11. Waterloo, ON: Wilfrid Laurier University Press.

Linke, Bernhard 2003. "Emotionalität und Status: Zur gesellschaftlichen Funktion von supplicationes und lectisternia in der römischen Republik." In: Kneppe, Alfred and Metzler, Dieter (eds), *Die emotionale Dimension antiker Religiösität.* Münster: Ugarit. 65–86.

Lubtchansky, Natacha and Pouzadoux, Claude 2008. "Montrer l'invisible: Introduction." In: Estienne, Sylvie et al. (eds), *Image et religion dans l'antiquité Gréco-Romaine: Actes du colloque de Rome, 11–13 décembre 2003.* Collection du Centre Jean Bérard 28. Naples: Centre Jean Bérard. 15–18.

Lucarelli, Ute 2007. *Exemplarische Vergangenheit: Valerius Maximus und die Konstruktion des sozialen Raumes in der frühen Kaiserzeit.* Hypomnemata 172. Göttingen: Vandenhoeck & Ruprecht.

Maar, Christa and Burda, Hubert (eds) 2004. *Iconic Turn: Die neue Macht der Bilder.* Cologne: DuMont.

MacBain, Bruce 1982. *Prodigy and Expiation: A Study in Religion and Politics in Republican Rome.* Collection Latomus 177. Brussels: Latomus.

Martin, Dale B. 2004. *Inventing Superstition: From the Hippocratics to the Christians.* Cambridge, MA: Harvard University Press.

Meyer, Birgit 2008. "Media and the Senses in the Making of Religious Experience: An Introduction." In: *Material Religion* 4. 124–35 (DOI: 10.2752/175183408X328262).

Minoja, Marco 2006. "Rituale funerario ed elementi di articolazione sociale a Capua in etá orientalizzante." In: Eles, Patrizia von (ed.), *La ritualità funeraria tra età del ferro e orientalizzante in Italia: Atti del Convegno Verucchio, 26–26 Giugno 2002*. Biblioteca Di "Studi Etruschi." Rome, Pisa: Istituto di Studi Etruschi. 121–9.

Mitchell, William J. T. 2005. *What Do Pictures Want? The Lives and Loves of Images*. Chicago, IL: University of Chicago Press.

Moellering, Arnim H. 1963. *Plutarch on Superstition: Plutarch's De Superstitione, its Place in the Changing Meaning of Deisidaimonia and in the Context of His Theological Writings*. Boston, MA: Christopher.

Mora, Fabio 1990. *Prosopografia Isiaca 1: Corpus prosopographicum religionis Isiacae*. EPRO 113. Leiden: Brill.

Moreschini, C. 1996. "Religione e filosofia in Plutarco." In: Gallo, Italo (ed.), *Plutarca e la religione*. Naples: D'Auria. 29–48.

Mouritsen, Henrik 1997. "Mobility and Social Change in Italian Towns during the Principate." In: Parkins, Helen M. (ed.), *Roman Urbanism: Beyond the Consumer City*. London: Routledge. 59–82.

Münz-Manor, Ophir 2013. "Narrating Salvation: Verbal Sacrifices in Late Antique Liturgical Poetry." In: Dohrmann, Natalie B. and Reed, Annette Yoshiko (eds), *Jews, Christians, and the Roman Empire*. Philadelphia, PA: University of Pennsylvania Press. 154–66.

Mylonopoulos, J. 2010. "Divine Images *versus* Cult Images: An Endless Story about Theories, Methods, and Terminologies." In: Mylonopoulos, J. (ed.), *Divine Images and Human Imaginations in Ancient Greece and Rome*. Leiden: Brill. 1–19.

Neusner, Jacob 1991. *The Mishnah: A New Translation*. New Haven, CT: Yale University Press.

North, John 2000. "Prophet and Text in the Third Century BC." In: Bispham, Edward and Smith, Christopher (eds), *Religion in Archaic and Republican Rome and Italy: Evidence and Experience*. Edinburgh: Edinburgh University Press. 92–107.

Orlin, Eric M. 2007. "Augustan Religion and the Reshaping of Roman Memory." In: *Arethusa* 40.1. 73–92.

Ornan, Tallay 2005. *The Triumph of the Symbol: Pictorial Representation of Deities in Mesopotamia and the Biblical Image Ban*. Orbis biblicus et orientalis 213. Göttingen: Vandenhoeck & Ruprecht.

Otto, Bernd-Christian 2011. *Magie: Rezeptions- und diskursgeschichtliche Analysen von der Antike bis zur Neuzeit*. Religionsgeschichtliche Versuche und Vorarbeiten 57. Berlin: de Gruyter.

Ouwerkerk, Coenraad A. J. van 1987. "'Effigies Dei' and the Religious Imagination: A Psychological Perspective." In: Plas, Dirk van der (ed.), *Effigies Dei: Essays on the History of Religions*. Leiden: Brill. 156–70.

Perrin, Robin D. 2001. "When Religion Becomes Deviance: Introducing Religion in Deviance and Social Problems Courses." In: *Teaching Sociology* 29. 134–52.

Petsalis-Diomidis, Alexia 2005. "The Body in Space: Visual Dynamics in Graeco-Roman Healing Pilgrimage." In: Elsner, Jas and Rutherford, Ian (eds), *Pilgrimage in Graeco-Roman and Early Christian Antiquity: Seeing the Gods*. Oxford: Oxford University Press. 183–218.

Pezzoli-Olgiati, Daria 2011. "Images in Images: Self-Reflexivity in Votive Paintings from the 19th Century." In: Pezzoli-Olgiati, Daria and Rowland, Christopher (eds), *Approaches to the Visual in Religion*. Research in Contemporary Religion. Göttingen: Vandenhoeck & Ruprecht. 21–38.

Phillips III, C. Robert 1991. "Nullum Crimen sine Lege: Socioreligious Sanctions on Magic." In Faraone, Christopher A. and Obbink, Dirk (eds), *Magika Hiera: Ancient Greek Magic and Religion*. New York, NY: Oxford University Press. 260–76.

— 1994. "Seek and Go Hide: Literary Source Problems and Graeco-Roman Magic." In: *Helios* 21.2. 107–14.

Pieper, Irene, Schimmelpfennig, Michael, and Soosten, Joachim von 2003. *Hä resien: Religionshermeneutische Studien zur Konstruktion von Norm und Abweichung*. Munich: Fink.

Pirenne-Delforge, Vinciane and Prescendi, Francesca 2011. *Nourrir les dieux? Sacrifice et representation du divin*. Actes de la VIe rencontre du Groupe de Recherche Europeén. "FIGURA. Représentation du Divin dans les Sociétés Grecque et Romaine" (Liège University, 23–24 October 2009). Translated by Groupe de Recherche Europeén, Figura, Kernos: Supplement, 26. Liège: Centre International d'Étude de la Religion Grecque Antique.

Raja, Rubina and Rüpke, Jörg (eds) 2015. *A Companion to the Archaeology of Religion in the Ancient World*. Boston, MA: Wiley-Blackwell.

Rawson, Elisabeth 1973. "The Interpretation of Cicero's 'De legibus'." In: Temporini, Hildegard (ed.), *Von den Anfängen Roms bis zum Ausgang der Republik*. Berlin: de Gruyter. 334–56.

Reed, Annette Yoshiko 2003. "'Jewish Christianity' after the 'Parting of the Ways': Approaches to Historiography and Self-Definition in the Pseudo-Clementines." In: Becker, Adam and Reed, Annette Yoshiko (eds), *The Ways that Never Parted: Jews and Christians in Late Antiquity and the Early Middle Ages*. Texts and Studies in Ancient Judaism / Texte und Studien zum Antiken Judentum 95. Tübingen: Mohr Siebeck. 189–231.

Riposati, Benedetto 1974 (1939–47). *M. Terenti Varronis De vita popvli Romani: Fonti, esegesi*. Edizione critica dei frammenti. Milan: Celuc.

Romaine, Suzanne 1989. *Bilingualism*. Language in Society 13. Oxford: Blackwell.

Rosenberger, Veit 1998. *Gezähmte Götter: Das Prodigienwesen der römischen Republik*. HABES 27. Stuttgart: Steiner.

— 2003. "Die verschwundene Leiche: Überlegungen zur Auffindung des Sarkophags Numas im Jahre 181 v. Chr." In: Kranemann, Benedikt and Rüpke, Jörg (eds), *Das Gedächtnis des Gedächtnisses: Zur Präsenz von Ritualen in beschreibenden und reflektierenden Texten*. Marburg: Diagonal. 39–59.

— 2005. "Prodigien aus Italien: Geographische Verteilung und religiöse Kommunikation." In: *Cahiers Glotz* 16. 235–57.

(ed.) 2013a. *Divination in the Ancient World: Religious Options and the Individual.* Potsdamer altertumswissenschaftliche Beiträge 46. Stuttgart: Steiner.

2013b. "Individuation through Divination: The hieroi logoi of Aelius Aristides." In: Rosenberger, Veit (ed.), *Divination in the Ancient World: Religious Options and the Individual.* Potsdamer altertumswissenschaftliche Beiträge 46. Stuttgart: Steiner. 153–73.

Rüpke, Jörg 1990. *Domi militiae: Die religiöse Konstruktion des Krieges in Rom.* Stuttgart: Steiner.

1992. "Wer las Caesars bella als commentarii?" In: *Gymnasium* 99. 201–26.

1994. "Ovids Kalenderkommentar: Zur Gattung der Libri fastorum." In: *Antike und Abendland* 40. 125–36.

1995. *Kalender und Öffentlichkeit: Die Geschichte der Repräsentation und religiösen Qualifikation von Zeit in Rom.* Religionsgeschichtliche Versuche und Vorarbeiten 40. Berlin: de Gruyter.

2003. "L'histoire des fasti romains: Aspects médiatiques." In: *Revue historique de droit français et étranger* 81. 125–39.

2005a [2007]. "Divination et décisions politiques dans la République romaine." In: *Cahiers Glotz* 16. 217–33.

2005b. "Varro's tria genera theologiae: Religious Thinking in the Late Republic." In: *Ordia prima* 4. 107–29.

2006a. *Die Religion der Römer. Eine Einführung.* Munich: Beck.

2006b. "Communicating with the Gods." In: Morstein-Marx, Robert and Rosenstein, Nathan (eds), *The Blackwell Companion to the Roman Republic.* Oxford: Blackwell. 215–35.

2006c. "Religion in lex Ursonensis." In: Ando, Clifford and Rüpke, Jörg (eds), *Religion and Law in Classical and Christian Rome.* Potsdamer altertumswissenschaftliche Beiträge. Alte Geschichte 15. Stuttgart: Steiner. 34–46.

2006d. "Urban Religion and Imperial Expansion: Priesthoods in the Lex Ursonensis." In: de Blois, Lukas, Funke, Peter, and Hahn, Johannes (eds), *The Impact of Imperial Rome on Religions, Ritual and Religious Life in the Roman Empire.* Proceedings of the fifth workshop of the international network Impact of Empire (Roman Empire, 200 BC – AD 476), Münster, 30 June – 4 July 2004. Leiden: Brill. 11–23.

2007a. *Historische Religionswissenschaft: Eine Einführung.* Religionswissenschaft heute 5. Stuttgart: Kohlhammer.

2007b. *Religion of the Romans.* Tr. and ed. by Richard Gordon. Cambridge: Polity Press.

2007c. "Roman Religion: Religions of Rome." In: Rüpke, Jörg (ed.), *A Companion to Roman Religion.* Malden, MA: Blackwell. 1–9.

(ed.) 2007d. *Antike Religionsgeschichte in räumlicher Perspektive: Abschlussbericht zum Schwerpunktprogramm 1080 der Deutschen Forschungsgemeinschaft "Römische Reichsreligion und Provinzialreligion".* Tübingen: Mohr Siebeck.

2007e. *Gruppenreligionen im römischen Reich: Sozialformen, Grenzziehungen und Leistungen.* Studien und Texte zu Antike und Christentum 43. Tübingen: Mohr Siebeck.

2008. *Fasti Sacerdotum: A Prosopography of Pagan, Jewish, and Christian Religious Officials in the City of Rome, 300 BC to AD 499.* Tr. by David M. B. Richardson. Oxford: Oxford University Press.

2009a. "Between Rationalism and Ritualism: On the Origins of Religious Discourse in the Late Roman Republic." In: *Archiv für Religionsgeschichte* 11. 123–43.

2009b. "Der Gott und seine Statue (Prop. 4.2): Kollektive und individuelle Repräsentationsstrategien in antiken Religionen." In: *Gymnasium* 116. 121–34.

2009c. "Properz: Aitiologische Elegie in Augusteischer Zeit." In: Bendlin, Andreas and Rüpke, Jörg (eds), *Römische Religion im historischen Wandel: Diskursentwicklung von Plautus bis Ovid.* Stuttgart: Steiner. 115–42.

2009d. "Religiöser Pluralismus und das römische Reich." In: Cancik, Hubert and Rüpke, Jörg (eds), *Die Religion des Imperium Romanum: Koine und Konfrontationen.* Tübingen: Mohr Siebeck. 331–54.

2010a. "Hellenistic and Roman Empires and Euro-Mediterranean Religion." In: *Journal of Religion in Europe* 3. 197–214.

2010b. "Radikale im öffentlichen Dienst: Status und Individualisierung unter römischen Priestern republikanischer Zeit." In: Barceló, Pedro (ed.), *Religiöser Fundamentalismus in der römischen Kaiserzeit.* Potsdamer altertumswissenschaftliche Beiträge 29. Stuttgart: Steiner. 11–21.

2011a. "Rationalité grecque et société romaine: Contextes politiques et intellectuels de la religion de la République tardive." In: Prescendi, Francesca and Volokhine, Youri (eds), *Dans le laboratoire de l'historien des religions: Mélanges offerts à Philippe Borgeaud.* Religions en perspective 24. Geneva: Labor et fides. 385–405.

2011b. *The Roman Calendar from Numa to Constantine: Time, History, and the Fasti.* Tr. by David M. B. Richardson. Boston, MA: Wiley-Blackwell.

2011c. "Divination romaine et rationalité grecque dans la Rome du deuxième siècle av. n.è." In: Georgoudi, Stella, Koch-Piettre, Renée, and Schmidt, Francis (eds), *Signes, rites et destin dans les sociétés de la Méditerranée ancienne.* Religions in the Graeco-Roman World 174. Leiden: Brill. 479–500.

2012a. *Religion in Republican Rome: Rationalization and Ritual Change.* Philadelphia, PA: University of Pennsylvania Press.

2012b. *Religiöse Erinnerungskulturen: Formen der Geschichtsschreibung in der römischen Antike.* Darmstadt: Wissenschaftliche Buchgesellschaft.

2013a. "Individuals and Networks." In: Bricault, Laurent and Bonnet, Corinne (eds), *Panthée: Religious Transformations in the Graeco-Roman Empire.* Religions in the Graeco-Roman World 177. Leiden: Brill. 261–77.

(ed.) 2013b. *The Individual in the Religions of the Ancient Mediterranean.* Oxford: Oxford University Press.

2013c. "Introduction: Individualisation and Individuation as Concepts for Historical Research." In: Rüpke, Jörg (ed.), *The Individual in the Religions of the Ancient Mediterranean.* Oxford: Oxford University Press. 3–28.

2014a. *From Jupiter to Christ: The History of Religion in the Roman Imperial Period.* Tr. by David M. B. Richardson. Oxford: Oxford University Press.

2014b. *Religion: Antiquity and its Legacy*. London/New York: Tauris/Oxford University Press.

2014c. "Historicizing Religion: Varro's Antiquitates and History of Religion in the Late Roman Republic." In: *History of Religions* 53.3. 246–68 (DOI: 10.1086/674241).

2015a. "Religious Agency, Identity, and Communication: Reflecting on History and Theory of Religion." In: *Religion* 45.3. 344–366 (DOI: 10.1080/0048721X.2015.1024040).

2015b. "Knowledge of Religion in Valerius Maximus' Exempla: Roman Historiography and Tiberian Memory Culture." In: Galinsky, Karl (ed.), *Roman Memory*. Oxford: Oxford University Press. 89–111.

Rüpke, Jörg and Spickermann, Wolfgang (eds) 2012. *Reflections on Religious Individuality: Greco-Roman and Judaeo-Christian Texts and Practices*. Religionsgeschichtliche Versuche und Vorarbeiten 62. Berlin: de Gruyter.

Rüpke, Jörg and Woolf, Greg (eds) 2013. *Religious Dimensions of the Self in the Second Century* CE. Studien und Texte zu Antike und Christentum 76. Tübingen: Mohr Siebeck.

Santangelo, Federico 2013. *Divination, Prediction and the End of the Republic*. Cambridge: Cambridge University Press.

Sauer, Eberhard 2003. *The Archaeology of Religious Hatred in the Roman and Early Medieval World*. Stroud: Tempus.

Sauer, Jochen 2007. *Argumentations- und Darstellungsformen im ersten Buch von Ciceros Schrift "De legibus"*. Heidelberg: Winter.

Sauron, Gilles 1994. *Quis deum? L'expression plastique des idéologies politiques et religieuses à Rome à la fin de la république et au début du principat*. Bibliothèque des Écoles françaises d'Athènes et de Rome 285. Rome: École française.

Schäfer, Peter 1997. *Judeophobia: Attitudes toward the Jews in the Ancient World*. Cambridge, MA: Harvard University Press.

Scheid, John 1981. "Le délit religieux dans la Rome tardo-républicaine." In: Scheid, John (ed.), *Le délit religieux dans la cité antique*. Rome: Ecole française. 117–71.

1985. *Religion et piété à Rome*. Paris: Découverte. 2nd edn. 2001.

1998. *La religion des Romains*. Paris: Armand Colin.

2013. *Les dieux, l'état et l'individu: Réflexions sur la religion civique à Rome*. Paris: Seuil.

Scheidel, Walter 2001. *Debating Roman Demography*. Leiden: Brill.

Schlette, Magnus and Jung, Matthias 2005. *Anthropologie der Artikulation: Begriffliche Grundlagen und transdisziplinäre Perspektiven*. Würzburg: Königshausen & Neumann.

Schmidt, Francis 1987. "Polytheisms: Degeneration or Progress?" In: *History and Anthropology* 3. 9–60.

Schmidt, Peter Lebrecht 1969. *Die Abfassungszeit von Ciceros Schrift über die Gesetze*. Collana di Studi Ciceroniani 4. Rome: Centro di Studi Ciceroniani.

Schörner, Günther 2003. *Votive im römischen Griechenland: Untersuchungen zur späthellenistischen und kaiserzeitlichen Kunst- und Religionsgeschichte*. Altertumswissenschaftliches Kolloquium 7. Stuttgart: Steiner.

Schröder, Bianca 2012. "Römische pietas: Kein universelles Postulat." In: *Gymnasium* 119.4. 335–58.

Schröter, Robert 1963. "Die varronische Etymologie." In: *Varro: Entretiens sur l'antiquité-classique* 9, Vandœvres-Genève (Fondation Hardt). 79–116.

Setaioli, Aldo 2007. "Seneca and the Divine: Stoic Tradition and Personal Developments." In: *International Journal of the Classical Tradition* 13.3. 333–68.

2013. "Cicero and Seneca on the Fate of the Soul: Private Feelings and Philosophical Doctrines." In: Rüpke, Jörg (ed.), *The Individual in the Religions of the Ancient Mediterranean*. Oxford: Oxford University Press. 455–88.

Sizgorich, Thomas 2009. *Violence and Belief in Late Antiquity: Militant Devotion in Christianity and Islam*. Philadelphia, PA: University of Pennsylvania Press.

Skidmore, Clive [Julian] 1996. *Practical Ethics for Roman Gentlemen: The Work of Valerius Maximus*. Exeter: University of Exeter Press.

Smith, Stephen A. 2008. "Introduction." In: Smith, Steven and Knight, Allan (eds), *Religion of Fools? Superstition Past and Present*. Past & Present Supplement N.S. 3. Oxford: Oxford University Press. 7–55.

Smith, Stephen A. and Knight, Allan (eds) 2008. *Religion of Fools? Superstition Past and Present*. Past & Present Supplement N.S. 3. Oxford: Oxford University Press.

Solmsen, Friedrich 1944. "Cicero on Religio and Superstitio." In: *Classical Weekly* 37.14. 159–60.

Stähli, Adrian 2002. "Bild und Bildakte in der griechischen Antike." In: Belting, Hans, Kamper, Dietmar, and Schulz, Martin (eds), *Quel Corps? Eine Frage der Repräsentation*. Munich: Wilhelm Fink Verlag. 67–84.

Steiner, Deborah Tarn 2001. *Images in Mind: Statues in Archaic and Classical Greek Literature and Thought*. Princeton, NJ: Princeton University Press.

Steinsapir, Ann Irvine 2005. *Rural Sanctuaries in Roman Syria: The Creation of a Sacred Landscape*. BAR International Series 1431. Oxford: Hedges.

Stek, Tesse D. 2009. *Cult Places and Cultural Change in Republican Italy: A Contextual Approach to Religious Aspects of Rural Society after the Roman Conquest*. Amsterdam Archaeological Studies 14. Amsterdam: Amsterdam University Press.

Stern, Sacha 2012. *Calendars in Antiquity: Empires, States, and Societies*. New York, NY: Oxford University Press.

Steuernagel, Dirk 2009. "Hafenstädte: Knotenpunkte religiöser Mobilität?" In: Bonnet, Corinne, Ribichini, Sergio, and Steuernagel, Dirk (eds), *Religioni in contatto nel Mediterraneo antico: Modalità di diffusione e processi di interferenza*. Actes de colloque (Como, May 2006) = *Mediterranea 4*. Pisa: Fabrizio Serra. 121–33.

Stewart, Peter 2003. *Statues in Roman Society: Representation and Response*. Oxford: Oxford University Press.

Stolz, Fritz 2004. *Religion und Rekonstruktion: Ausgewählte Aufsätze*. Göttingen: Vandenhoeck & Ruprecht.

Störling, Gustav 1894. *Quaestiones Ciceronianae ad religionem spectantes*. Diss. Jena.

Stroumsa, Guy G. 2008. "The End of Sacrifice: Religious Mutations of Late Antiquity." In: Misset-van de Weg, Magda (ed.), *Empsuchoi Logoi: Festschrift Pieter van der Horst*. Leiden: Brill. 29–46.

2009. *The End of Sacrifice: Religious Transformations in Late Antiquity*. Chicago, IL: University of Chicago Press.

Stuckrad, Kocku von 2006. "Visual Gods: From Exorcism to Complexity in Renaissance Studies." In: *Aries* 6.1. 59–85.

Tanaseanu-Döbler, Ilinca 2009. "'Nur der Weise ist Priester': Rituale und Ritualkritik bei Porphyrios." In: Berner, Ulrich and Tanaseanu-Döbler, Ilinca (eds), *Religion und Kritik in der Antike*. Religionen in der pluralen Welt 7. Münster: LIT. 109–55.

Tellegen-Couperus, Olga (ed.) 2012. *Law and Religion in the Roman Republic*. Mnemosyne Supplement 336. Leiden: Brill.

Thio, Alex, Calhoun, Thomas H., and Conyers, Adrian 2008. "Introduction." In: Thio, Alex, Calhoun, Thomas H., and Conyers, Adrian (eds), *Readings in Deviant Behavior*. Boston, MA: Pearson. 1–8.

Todisco, L. 2005. "Bambini, fanciulli e dediche votive in Italia meridionale." In: Comella, A. and Mele, S. (eds), *Depositi votivi e culti dell'Italia antica a quella tardo-Repubblicana*. Bari: Edipuglia. 713–21.

Toorn, Karel van der 2008. "Votive Texts and Letter-Prayers: Writing as Devotional Practice." In: Spek, R. J. van der (ed.), *Studies in Ancient Near Eastern World View and Society*. Bethesda, MD: CDL Press. 39–46.

Turpin, José 1986. "Cicéron, De legibus I–II et la religion romaine: Une interprétation philosophique à la veille du principat." *ANRW* II.16.3. 1877–908.

Uehlinger, Christoph 2006. "Visible Religion und die Sichtbarkeit von Religion(en): Voraussetzungen, Anknüpfungsprobleme, Wiederaufnahme eines religionswissenschaftlichen Forschungsprogramms." In: *Berliner Theologische Zeitschrift* 23.2. 165–84.

Ullucci, Daniel C. 2012. *The Christian Rejection of Animal Sacrifice*. Oxford: Oxford University Press.

Van den Bruwaene, Marcel 1961. "Précisions sur la loi religieuse du de legibus II 19–22 de Cicéron." In: *Helikon* 1. 40–93.

Van Nuffelen, Peter 2011. *Rethinking the Gods: Philosophical Readings of Religion in the Post-Hellenistic Period*. Cambridge: Cambridge University Press.

Van Straten, F. T. 1981. "Gifts for the Gods." In: Versnel, Hendrik S. (ed.), *Faith, Hope and Worship: Aspects of Religious Mentality in the Ancient World*. Leiden: Brill. 65–151.

Versnel, Hendrik S. 1987. "What Did Ancient Man See When He Saw a God? Some Reflections on Greco-Roman Epiphany." In: Plas, Dirk van der (ed.), *Effigies Dei: Essays on the History of Religions*. Leiden: Brill. 42–55.

Vigourt, Annie 2011. "Normes religieuses et piété privée vers le milieu du IIe siècle ap. J.-C." In: Cabouret-Laurioux, Bernadette and Charles-Laforge, Marie-Odile (eds), *La norme religieuse dans l'antiquité*. Paris: De Boccard. 73–84.

Vinzent, Markus 2014. *Marcion and the Dating of the Synoptic Gospels*. Studia patristica suppl. 2. Leuven: Peeters.

Wallraff, Martin 2003. "Viele Metaphern – viele Götter? Beobachtungen zum Monotheismus in der Spätantike." In: Frey, Jörg, Rohls, Jan, and Zimmermann, Ruben (eds), *Metaphorik und Christologie*. Berlin: de Gruyter. 151–66.

Wardle, D. 1998. *Valerius Maximus, Memorable Deeds and Sayings Book 1*. Tr. with Introd. and Comm. Oxford: Clarendon.

Walker, Henry John 2004. *Valerius Maximus, Memorable Deeds and Sayings: One Thousand Tales from Ancient Rome*. Tr. with Introd. Indianapolis, IN: Hackett.

Wifstrand Schiebe, Marianne 2003. "Sind die Epikureischen Götter 'thought-constructs'?" In: *Mnemosyne* 56.6. 703–27.

Wissowa, Georg 1912. *Religion und Kultus der Römer*. 2nd edn. Handbuch der Altertumswissenschaft 5.4 Munich: Beck.

Woolf, Greg 2013. "Ritual and the Individual in Roman Religion." In: Rüpke, Jörg (ed.), *The Individual in the Religions of the Ancient Mediterranean*. Oxford: Oxford University Press. 136–60.

Wrede, Henning 1981. *Consecratio in formam deorum: Vergöttlichte Privatpersonen in der römischen Kaiserzeit*. Mainz: Philipp von Zabern.

Yuval, Israel Jacob, Harshav, Barbara, and Chipman, Jonathan 2008. *Two Nations in your Womb: Perceptions of Jews and Christians in Late Antiquity and the Middle Ages*. Mark Taper Foundation Book in Jewish Studies. Berkeley, CA: University of California Press.

Zeddies, Nicole 2003. *Religio et sacrilegium: Studien zur Inkriminierung von Magie, Häresie und Heidentum (4.–7. Jahrhundert)*. Europäische Hochschulschriften Reihe 3, Geschichte und ihre Hilfswissenschaften. Frankfurt am Main: Lang.

Zevi, Fausto 1987. "I santuari di Roma agli inizi della repubblica." In: Cristofani, Mauro (ed.), *Etruria e Lazio arcaico*. Rome: Consiglio Nazionale delle Ricerche. 121–32.

Zinser, Hartmut 2002. "Religio, Secta, Haeresis in den Häresiegesetzen des Codex Theodosianus (16.5.1/66) von 438." In: Hutter, Manfred (ed.), *Hairesis: Festschrift für Karl Hoheisel zum 65. Geburtstag*. Münster: Aschendorff. 215–19.

Index locorum

Subject index